A PLACE
AT THE
TABLE

40 Days of Solidarity with the Poor

CHRIS SEAY

BakerBooks

a division of Baker Publishing Group
Grand Rapids, Michigan

Published by Baker Books
a division of Baker Publishing Group
P.O. Box 6287, Grand Rapids, MI 49516-6287
www.bakerbooks.com

Printed in the United States of America

Library of Congress Cataloging-in-Publication Data
Seay, Chris.
    A place at the table : 40 days of solidarity with the poor / Chris Seay.
        p.   cm.
    Includes bibliographical references (p.   ).
    ISBN 978-0-8010-1451-2 (pbk.)
    1. Fasting—Religious aspects—Christianity. 2. Poverty—Religious aspects—Christianity. I. Title
    BV5055.54 2012
    248.47—dc23   2011038215

14   15   16   17   18   8   7   6   5

In memory of my grandfather
Robert Steele Baldwin (Bro. Bob).
For sixty years you served the church as a pastor,
taught me about the radical love of Jesus, and lived
out the best sermon ever preached. I miss you so much,
but I know that heaven is your greatest delight.

When the poor meet the rich,
riches will have no meaning.
And when the rich meet the poor,
we will see poverty come to an end.

—Shane Claiborne

Contents

Acknowledgments

To my family: Lisa, Hanna, Trinity, Solomon, and Christian, you make life so much fun.

I am so grateful for siblings who are my dearest friends: Brian, Jennifer, Robbie, and Jessica, you are the best.

Ecclesia, it is a privilege to serve you as we strive to see the gospel of our Liberating King change the world. Thank you for believing in miracles and looking for the best in other people. I am so grateful to Steven Hicks, Elizabeth Cook, and Wayne Brown for helping me lead within my strengths. I love you all!

Many thanks to Mark Lanier and the dedicated staff at the Lanier Theological Library. I consider the library and chapel to be the Eighth Wonder of the World and feel so blessed to read, write, study, and pray in this sacred place.

Kelly Hall, I am so grateful for your help on this project.

My amazing agent, Esther Fedorkevich: I am grateful for your partnership on this and many future projects.

To my editor: Chad Allen, it has been a joy working with you. I am also grateful to all of the amazing people at Baker.

Rick McKinley, Greg Holder, and all the Advent Conspirators, I pray that we all continue to Worship Fully, Spend Less, Give More, and Love All!

Ecclesia Bible Society and all the team working on *The Voice*: your hard work in bringing the Scriptures to life for those who may have never heard this good news is forever appreciated.

Foreword

Dare to Discover

I always thought issues like poverty and orphans were too big for me to get involved. Too far removed. Too expensive and complicated. Too daunting for my stage of life.

I was an overwhelmed white girl trying to navigate being a wife and mom to three little people. I was compassionate, but I was distracted. I reasoned there would be a time for me to think beyond my own mailbox eventually, but not now.

That is, until God brought Africa to my doorstep.

It was an ordinary day in my rush-and-hurry life. My girls were giddy with excitement over our scheduled outing with my middle daughter's Brownie troop. In the midst of slapping sandwiches on the table and throwing hair bows on the ends of three little tangled ponytails, I grabbed a world map and quipped, "Liberia. That's where this choir that we're going to hear today is from. It's a country in South America, kids. Let's find it."

We looked and looked. Then my oldest daughter, nine at the time, said, "Um, Mom, I'm pretty sure Liberia is this little country over here—on the west coast of Africa."

"Absolutely. I just wanted to make sure you were paying attention."

Off we went on this ordinary day to an ordinary church in the middle of our ordinary town. We sat in an ordinary pew and felt nothing but ordinary.

Until. Until the extraordinary presence of God invaded that very ordinary place. God brought Africa, the orphans, the poverty, the reality, very close. Too close to ignore. Too close to deny. Too close to walk away. Too close to stay wrapped up in my ordinary life.

I couldn't do everything, but I could do something.

Our family's something wound up being a wonderfully crazy adventure of making a place at our table for two African choir boys who became our sons through adoption. And while adoption can be wonderful, it's not the only way to make a place at the table. It's not the only way to let God interrupt the ruts of normal. The normal that keeps us distracted and blinded and without expectation of something more. But one thing is certain: the something more we're made to experience with God can only be found outside the ruts.

So here's my challenge. Are you willing to stay out of the rut of normal for 40 days? Are you willing to mess with your normal patterns of eating in this 40-day adventure? It's biblical, but it's hard. It's worth it, but it will surely bump into your "happy" in many ways.

I know this to be true on a personal level. You know that Scripture about not twisting your face and sulking because you're fasting? Yes, well, that's a hard one for me.

I recently did an extended fast from sugar and soda. At certain points of my journey, I wanted something sweet and something with fizz so badly I felt I should wear a T-shirt: "I'm fasting from sugar and soda. Talk to me at your own risk."

Lovely. That sort of defeats the whole spiritual growth part of fasting, right? But, let's be honest, leaving the rut of normal isn't easy.

The book you're holding, written by my friend Chris Seay, is a realistic, honest, and compassionate treasure. Anyone escaping the rut of normal through fasting will appreciate Chris's spiritual depth along with his transparency about being human.

10

We will come to our wit's end during this fast. Some of us will blow it. But Chris reminds us this journey isn't about our power, strength of character, or self-control. It is a journey of surrender to God that will usher us from rut dwelling to transformed living.

In the process of being transformed, we will become more and more aware not just of our hunger but of the hunger of the world.

We will sit down at the table more eager to ponder those we might serve instead of pouncing on the plenty to which we've grown so accustomed. So very tragically accustomed. God help us.

A place at the table. Indeed, a place at the table for God and for remembering those less fortunate. But even more so, a place to stop the rut of constant inhale. Taking in, taking in, taking in. It clogs the soul. So for 40 days, let us learn to exhale with great thanksgiving. Thankful for Africa coming close. For pondering what God might bring close during this fast. For this place where our souls breathe and dream once again.

Lysa Terkeurst

Introduction

An Invitation to a Life-Changing Journey

Do you wish your prayer to fly towards God? Give it two wings:
fasting and almsgiving.

—Augustine of Hippo

Early in 2011, I was blessed to travel to the Holy Land and sit
for hours just outside Jericho atop Mount Quarantania (which
in Latin means "forty"), named for the 40 days Jesus fasted in
preparation for His ministry. This mountain and its surroundings
are where Jesus wandered during His days of fasting, contemplation, and temptation. Looking out over the wild, I was awakened
to the severity of Jesus's fast. This area provides no shelter, very
little shade, no natural water source, and obviously no food. I
imagined the almighty God of the universe staggering through
this land—alone, hot, tired, and hungry.

Why on earth would God Himself embrace a season of fasting?
It might be because He knows some deep truths about the world
and about humanity. God's decision again and again to give up
His power—from when He came to earth in the form of a crying
baby, to when He fasted in the desert, to when He allowed people
to torture and execute Him—teaches us something very important:

the world will not be changed when we ascend to power. God's kingdom will not be furthered because an evangelical Christian resides in the White House or the highest court in the land. God changes the world through humility and service. It is a subversive tactic, yet highly effective.

Just look back on the history of Christianity, and you can see it in the movements spawned by William Wilberforce, Martin Luther King Jr., or Dorothy Day. Lasting change may eventually be legislated and enforced, but it doesn't start there. It first takes root in the hearts of people. When God changes our hearts, a transforming love is unleashed on the world.

The same truth applies to each of us on a personal level. We will experience radical transformation in humility and service, not superiority and power. The primary reason why we struggle so deeply to be transformed into the character of Christ is likely because so often instead of living with humility and vulnerability, we are busy chasing power and prestige.

Can we embrace the truths of Christ if we do not embrace His posture? His hands were exposed to disease and leprosy as He touched the sick. His knee bent to the ground to wash the sullied feet of His friends. His eyes lifted in prayer to the Father. His body bowed and was broken in death. As we learn to march in step with our Savior, we find that our swagger gives way to a lowly and humble way of walking.

To be strong Christians, we must embrace weakness. It is when we accept our humanity, when we are humbled by our fallibility, when we live vulnerably, that God is strong within us. Jesus was lowly, humble, even despised. He did not seek comfort. He did not even have a place to lay His head. He had every opportunity to pursue power yet didn't. The world systems and its currency did not hold value for Jesus. He had a vision of a different sort of kingdom.

Fasting for 40 days has tremendous biblical significance. In fact, the number 40 is mentioned more than 120 times in the Scriptures. Moses spent 40 days on Mt. Sinai; Noah spent 40 days and nights afloat on the water. In the 40 days Jesus spent fasting in the wilderness, He seems to correct the failures of Israel and fulfill the hope of Isaiah 43:19, where it says:

> Watch *closely,* I am preparing something new; it's happen-
> ing now, *even as I speak,*
> and you're about to see it. I am preparing a way
> through the desert;
> Waters will flow where there had been none.

Can you imagine what God can accomplish in and through you if you offer Him 40 days of devotion?

Should you be willing, this book can help you discover and face your weaknesses and reveal the source of true strength. I invite you to set out to rediscover what the Bible says about food, life, love, and grace, and to connect with the poor. I invite you to join me on a 40-day fast. Let me clarify that when I say "fast," I do not mean going without food for 40 days. (If you try to do so, please consult with a physician beforehand.) For instance, when I did this fast during Lent in 2011, I chose to eat a diet very similar to that of the children our family sponsors in Uganda and Ecuador through Compassion International. (In chapter 3, I give some practical tips and ideas on ways to fast.)

Whenever I begin a fast, I do it in hopes of becoming a differ-ent man—a grateful man. It is my greatest hope that through our willingness to be vulnerable, to be changed, to be active agents of hope in a world that so desperately needs it, we will encounter the Risen Christ together and be renewed and changed forever.

Will you join me on this journey?

A Word about *The Voice* Bible Translation

I use *The Voice* translation of the Bible throughout this book. *The Voice* is a project of the Ecclesia Bible Society, which assembled a collective of creatives and scholars to write a translation that is not only accurate in its meaning but beautiful in its telling. In many ways the Bible is an artful collection of literary artifacts—poems, letters, parables, stories, proverbs. But many translations today focus so much on meaning that they leave out the artful expression. Getting the meaning right is very important, but I would argue that you lose some meaning, or you at least lose some of what the original texts intended, if the meaning you receive is bereft of its artful presentation. *The Voice* is the Ecclesia Bible Society's effort to recapture what has been lost.

The Voice uses two devices that may be unfamiliar. Italics indicate words that are not directly tied to the original language. The purpose of these italicized words is to convey information that would have been obvious to the original recipients. *The Voice* also employs a screenplay format to identify dialog and avoid repetition of simple conjunctions.

I hope this story-driven translation helps you to have a fresh and living interaction with God's Word.

1

From Consuming to Sharing

Embracing Our Ability to Change Things

Nothing is so inconsistent with the life of any Christian as over-indulgence.

—The Rule of Benedict

Freedom. It is a beautiful gift. As Christians, we know that Jesus came to free us from the law and the oppression that comes with religious regulations. We love to call out with the apostle Paul a slogan often quoted on these matters: "'*And* where the Spirit of the Lord is present, there is liberty.'"[1] And as Americans, we unapologetically make a spectacle of our freedom.

I have come to believe, however, that our Western understanding of freedom is not at all what Jesus came to bring us. We have allowed our love of freedom to become an excuse to live a life marked by self-absorbed consumerism.

I find it interesting that we use the term "consumption" not only for the act of eating but also the for goods we buy and use.

Definition of **CONSUME**
transitive verb
1: to do away with completely : destroy <fire *consumed* several buildings>
2 a : to spend wastefully : squander
b : use up <writing *consumed* much of his time>
3 a : to eat or drink especially in great quantity <*consumed* several bags of pretzels>
b : to enjoy avidly : devour <mysteries, which she *consumes* for fun—E. R. Lipson>
4: to engage fully : engross <*consumed* with curiosity>
5: to utilize as a customer <*consume* goods and services>
intransitive verb
1: to waste or burn away : perish
2: to utilize economic goods[2]

As we obsess over the newest technology and the latest fashions, we find the majority of our income is spent on what we love most—ourselves—while the world is hurting.

- One billion people lack access to clean water, and 2.6 billion people lack basic sanitation.
- According to UNICEF, 22,000 children die each day due to extreme poverty.
- Out of 2.2 billion children in the world, 1 billion live in poverty.[3]
- The wealthiest nation on earth has the widest gap between rich and poor of any industrialized nation.[4]

As Christians who are called to love the least of these, we need to realize that poverty is not just *a* problem, it is *our* problem. When we contemplate what is happening globally, we might likely agree that a large percentage of our income should be diverted immediately to care for those in greatest need. We could easily determine that 50 percent or more of our annual income should be given away.

After all, if 80 percent of the world lives on less than $10 a day,[5] surely we could survive on some multiple of that number. But the challenge comes when we try to transition from sharing a very small percentage of our income to radical generosity. We face bills, rent, student loans, luxurious habits, long commutes, and scores of other problems that overwhelm us and often translate to a shut down, and we change nothing about our lifestyles at all.

We need to follow the example set for us by the people of God in Acts, who shared all that they had—a striking portrait of the church getting on her feet and discovering her unique identity. One of the church's shining features was her focus on sharing with anyone who had a need. It was as if Jesus had told them, "I will provide everything that you need; the only obstacle is that some of you will have too much and others will not have enough. I'm counting on you to sort it out."

This model did not start with Jesus; it goes all the way back to the Israelites and their life in the wilderness. Paul in his letters echoes the model offered to the children of Israel as an ethic for us all to live by. The kingdom is a place where everyone has enough.

In Exodus, God's plan for gathering manna is laid out:

> When they used a two-quart jar to measure it, the one who had gathered a lot didn't have more than he needed; and the one who gathered less had just what he needed. *Miraculously*, each person *and each family*—regardless of how much they gathered—had exactly what they needed.[6]

Paul explains to us that this lesson was not just for God's children in the wilderness:

> The objective is not to go under [financially speaking] so others will have some relief; the objective is to use this opportunity today to supply their needs out of your abundance. *One day it may be the other way around,* and they will need to supply your needs from what they have. That's equality. As it is written, "The one who gathered plenty didn't have more than he needed; the one who gathered little didn't have less."[7]

Our problem seems clear. We have not been sharing our manna equally.

The Scriptures prescribe a remedy to our consumerism and selfishness: fasting.

Listen to God speak to the prophet Isaiah:

Eternal One: No, what I want in a fast is this:
to liberate those tied down and held back by injustice,
to lighten the load of those heavily burdened,
to free the oppressed and shatter every type of oppression.
A fast *for Me* involves sharing your food with people who have none,
giving those who are homeless a space in your home,
Giving clothes to those who need them, and not neglecting your
own family.

Then, *oh then,* your light will break out like the *warm, golden rays of a*
rising sun;
in an instant, you will be healed.
Your rightness will precede *and protect* you;
the glory of the Eternal will follow and defend you.
Then when you do call out, *"My God, Where are You?"*
The Eternal One will answer, "I am here, *I am here."*
If you remove the yoke of oppression *from the downtrodden among*
you,
stop accusing others, and do away with mean and inflammatory
speech,
If you make sure that the hungry and oppressed have all that they
need,
then your light will shine in the darkness,
And even your bleakest moments will be bright as a clear day.[8]

The Shepherd of Hermas, a collection of Christian teachings from AD 150, suggests,

having fulfilled what is written, in the day on which you fast you
will taste nothing but bread and water; and having reckoned up the
price of the dishes of that day which you intended to have eaten,
you will give it to a widow, or an orphan, or to some person in

want, and thus you will exhibit humility of mind, so that he who has received benefit from your humility may fill his own soul, and pray for you to the Lord.[9]

Augustine said our fasting should always nourish the poor: "Break your bread for those who are hungry, said Isaiah, do not believe that fasting suffices. Fasting chastises you, but it does not refresh the other. Your privations shall bear fruit if you give generously to another."[10] In other words, if you pass on dinner, don't simply leave your plate in the cupboard; give your portion to someone who has none.

In the developing world, 28 percent of children are underweight or have stunted growth. In the industrialized world our problem is exactly the opposite. Obesity in children rises year by year. In 1980 fewer than one out of ten people were obese. This number has exploded; most recent surveys indicate one out of every two people is either overweight or obese.[11] It is not hard to do the math and know that what the world needs right now is for Christians in the industrialized world to take less and share more, as the passage from Isaiah demands. What can you and I do about it? I say we should take 40 days and participate in this kingdom experiment of taking only what we need and sharing the rest.

2

Miracle Bread

Nurturing Gratitude for God's Provision

Pride and a too-full stomach are old bed-fellows. . . . Fasting, then, is a divine corrective to the pride of the human heart. It is a discipline of the body with a tendency to humble the soul.

—Arthur Wallis, *God's Chosen Fast*

We often see ourselves most clearly in our children. I will never forget driving across town with my four-year-old son Solomon in the backseat. I could see he was deep in thought. As I watched him intently pondering what seemed to be a brilliant thought or mysterious question, I finally came right out and asked him: "Solomon, what are you thinking so hard about?" He looked up in an honest gaze and said simply, "Dad, I just been thinkin' 'bout how much I love dem waffles." I knew in that moment he was his father's son. Many days I wake up, and the first thought to enter my mind is, "What do I want to eat today?" I really like food, and here in Houston I have a lot of good choices. It's embarrassing to admit, but many mornings (even before the sun is completely up) I wonder whether to have Tex-Mex or Korean tacos. Or what about Thai cuisine, or Indian? It is not just the time I spend answering the question that makes me feel so self-absorbed, but also the way my cravings have the power to shape my day.

Certainly, our relationship with food is a unique window into our soul. In the days leading up to a fast I committed to a few years ago, a very simple realization broke my will, pride, and eventually my heart. I realized that the joy that food and material possessions bring to me is often substantial, but that far too often I lack any sense of gratitude for it. The fact that God sustains our lives by a gift from His hand should cause us to stop everything and offer sincere thanks, but so often we do not. The same is true for the air we breathe, our health and well-being, and sadly even the grace and forgiveness offered to us through Jesus the Liberating King.

We are not the first ones to lose a sense of appreciation and wonder at God's provision. The Israelites, after struggling and hungering in the wilderness, received God-given miracle bread that fell from the sky day after day. But, eventually, they lost sight of this amazing gift.

> The people griped *about life in the wilderness,* how hard they felt things were for them, and these *evil* complaints came up to the ears of the Eternal One. He was furious about this *ingratitude, faithlessness, and lack of vision.* His anger was kindled, and His fire raged among them and devoured some of the camp's perimeter.[1]

The Israelites sound like spoiled, lazy, ungrateful kids—a label that hits too close to home. We too have complained and will complain again when we get less than what we crave.

And let's face it, we all run into times when our menus get stale. "What? We're having spaghetti again?" We live in stimulating times, and it is no wonder our taste buds want in on the entertainment. And why not?

Near my church in downtown Houston is a bakery. I don't know anybody who can catch a scent of this place without their mouth watering. I imagine this smell filling the air as the children of Israel pat out their daily manna and cook it over the fire. But even that delicious bread would get tiresome day after day. The gathering, grinding, and patting. The going-nowhere, desert nomad existence of each day.

When did the miraculous provision of God become a burden to them? Was their dissatisfaction merely a result of boredom? For that matter, how can a miracle become so common in our own daily lives that we become apathetic and eventually unthankful? Ask a nurse who works in labor and delivery if the miracle of a child's birth becomes routine. The children of Israel started to long for different flavors and spices. They were so blinded by their cravings that they began to glorify the "good old days" of slavery when they could eat all they wanted.

A contingent of Israelites had a strong craving for different food, and the Israelites started complaining again.

Israelites: Who will give us meat to eat? Remember in Egypt when we could eat whatever amount of fish we wanted, or even the abundant cucumbers, melons, leeks, onions, and garlic. *But this, this can hardly be called food at all!* Our appetites have dried up. All we ever have to look at is manna, *manna, manna.*[2]

In Egypt the fish was free? Really?! They were slaves who worked hard all day, were beaten regularly, watched their children die, but fish was free? Are you kidding?

And then, God looked upon them, saying, "This was supposed to be a short trip—you are the ones who have extended it for 40 years with your disobedience."

The next part of the story is my favorite. As a pastor I identify with Moses. He was looking at these people, two million of them, standing in front of their tents whining. If you are a parent you know the torture of listening to one whining kid, so multiply that by two million, and you have a sense of what Moses was feeling as he called out to God. The people wanted meat, but Moses had no meat, so he turned to God, wondering, "What have I done to deserve these people?!" You have to love how he can speak so honestly to God. "What do You want me to do, breastfeed two million people? I am not up for it." (Can you hear the sarcasm?) Then God tells Moses to have the entire camp prepare to eat meat.

Well, Moses overheard the people in *all* the clans moaning at the door of their tents *about the manna*. The Eternal grew really angry *again*, and Moses thought *the whole situation* was wrong.

Moses *(to the Lord)*: Why are You so hard on me? *I am* Your *devoted* servant. Why don't You look on me with affection? Why do I have the great burden of these *spiteful* people? Did I conceive them, *bear them*, and give birth to them? Why should You tell me to carry them—as a nanny does some suckling infant—into the land that You swore to their ancestors? And now, where am I supposed to find meat to feed this crowd crying out that I give them food to eat? I simply cannot keep carrying them along. They are way too heavy. If You plan to treat me like this, then just kill me now. If You care about me at all, just put me out of my misery so I do not have to live out this distress.

Eternal One *(to Moses)*: Listen, just do this for Me. Get 70 community elders, ones whom you know are real leaders among the people, and bring them into the congregation tent where we meet. Tell them to stand with you there. I will then descend among you. I will speak with you, and withdraw some of My spirit from you and place it on them so that they can help you with the burden of this people. Then you won't have to carry it all alone. Then tell the people this: "Purify yourselves for what will happen tomorrow. You will eat meat because you have cried to Me, saying, 'If only someone would give us meat to eat! We were content back in Egypt.' The Eternal will indeed give you meat, and you shall eat it. You'll be eating *meat* not just one day, or two or five or ten or twenty, but *every single day* for an entire month. *Meat, meat, and more meat. You'll eat meat* until it comes out of your noses and you can't stand it anymore. For you've rejected Me, who is with you, by asking why you left Egypt."

Moses: There are 600,000 people walking with me here. You say that You're going to give them *heaps of* meat for an entire month? *Think of the logistics!* Are there really enough sheep and cattle traveling with

26

us to slaughter, or enough fish in the sea *for that matter,* to provide such a supply?

Eternal One: Do you doubt Me? Do you question My power, that I can do what I've said? Just watch—you'll see what will happen.[3]

God is being really clear: "I'll give you meat to eat, literally so much that you will vomit it up out of your nose." It's not pretty. And it gets even more over the top. Remember this: Numbers 11:23. Write it on your steering wheel, or better yet on your checkbook.

Eternal One: Do you doubt Me? Do you question My power, that I can do what I've said? Just watch—you'll see what will happen.[4]

Your struggles are not too big for God. Now, imagine you are standing out in the wilderness, and the wind begins to pick up.

Suddenly the Eternal One blew a wind carrying quails in from around the sea and letting them drop all around the camp. There were quails *as far as the eye could see*—a day's journey on one side of the camp and another day's journey on the other side, and they were about three feet deep on the ground. The people got to work *right away,* gathering the quails. It took them the rest of that day and all night and the entire next day *to pick up all the birds.* Finally, no one had fewer than 60 bushels, and they spread them out all over the camp. While the people were still biting meat *off the bone,* before it was even chewed, the anger of the Eternal was unleashed against them. He struck the people down with a terrible plague. *Because He killed so many of them* on account of their craving and these buried there, the place was called Kibroth-hattaavah, *which means "graves of cravings."* The people journeyed on from there to Hazeroth, where they stayed *for awhile.*[5]

The Israelites have been whining, whimpering, grumbling, and praying for meat, and here it comes—three feet high.

This story is a great reminder about what happens when we whine or, worse, pray for and receive what we want. Take a look around at your excess. Do you think a Lexus will make you happy?

That car may become your prison cell. We are thick with what we have begged for, and those things may not be blessings at all. They are more likely our curse—what the New Testament calls cravings that give birth to sin (James 1:15).

The Israelites got everything they wanted and more but literally died by overconsumption. Were the birds sick? Did the meat sit in the sun too long? Or did the wrath of God require that these complainers receive justice?

We could easily fall to the same fate. It is time that we stop whining and obsessing and take the courageous step of faith that is required if we are ever to know the land of promise.

The time has come to see the food set before us as manna—our miraculous provision for the day. Certainly, if you haven't grown it, gathered it, transported it, frozen it, or packaged it, it is a miracle that it makes it to your table. Avocados from Mexico become guacamole on a table in Minnesota in December? Amazing. But how can we learn to be grateful for the food placed before us? Is it possible—as we learn to live presently, as we seek each day to receive with satisfaction what we need—that we will find God has provided everything we need? I believe so.

3

Tools

Practical Steps for Fasting as a Sacred Journey

When you are fasting and feel hungry, you are to remember that
you are really hungry for God.

—Lauren Winner, *Mudhouse Sabbath*

Christianity is filled with truths that seem so paradoxical on
the surface: the last will be first, we must die in order to live,
in weakness we are made strong, the poor and persecuted will be
blessed. How can these things be?

I enjoy the feeling of strength, power, and security—not insecurity, vulnerability, and frailty. I like having enough money in my
account to cover my bills and groceries for months to come. But
the truth is, when I am satisfied with my life and provisions each
day, when I am not striving for a Ferrari or any version of my own
personal extravagance, and learn to trust God above myself, I am
better off.

Together we will discover the true strength of God as we walk His path of weakness. Along this journey, temptations will come. Satan waits until we are weak—and so part of our journey is about embracing our true need for God and allowing Him to fortify us. It won't be easy. But I want to offer a few suggestions on how we can make it more meaningful along the way.

Plan out your meals and remember the poor.

You may want to choose the diet of your sponsor children, a region the Lord has placed on your heart, or a place where friends serve as missionaries. There are many staple foods to choose from: bananas, potatoes, lentils, and others. Other ideas include surviving on what someone would get from food stamps or asking your local food bank if there is a limit on how much a person can take and working with that. Consider the list of ingredients, listen for guidance, set your budget, consult a physician or nutritionist if you feel you need to, and then write out your grocery list. Make it as convenient as you can. Some, for example, have found it useful to purchase a rice cooker. These foods are abundant in stores, of course, and most any restaurant, so you should always have enough food to eat. There is no reason to be overtired, undernourished, or faint. The primary change in your life will be what happens when you lay down the vain pursuit of constantly asking yourself, "What do I want to eat today?"

For my 2011 Lenten fast, I chose to eat a diet of staples similar to those my sponsor children eat: rice, beans, salad/veggies, and tortillas. Full disclosure: I also allowed myself to drink fair trade coffee. By embracing these meals I was embracing the children I sponsor. I am ashamed to say that too often I forget these children for extended periods of time between the letters we exchange. But eating the foods they eat for 40 days helps me make a place for them at my table and in my heart.

Make your fast count for those who are less fortunate. One way to do this is to subtract the value of what you eat during the fast from the value of what you normally eat, and give this amount to the poor.

Read the 40 daily readings found in this book.

I hope the readings will nourish you daily as you seek to live in solidarity with the poor. These readings are not about fasting, primarily. I wrote most of them during one of my own Lenten fasts and chose to focus them on the internal issues that fasting brings to the surface. As we contemplate the Israelites' exodus as well as Jesus' final exodus, we will ponder our own need for exodus—from the cares of consumerism to those of God; from manufactured needs to real ones; from accumulating more to giving more away.

At the end of each reading I will introduce you to some new friends to pray for, perhaps someone who doesn't have clean water or lives in a developing country lacking medical care, food, or a chance to go to school. Along the way we are going to connect to other people and stop thinking about ourselves.

Consult your calendar.

Lent is a great time to participate in this fast. It is a time of preparation for the highest holy day in the Christian calendar, Easter. Holy Week and Easter are so important to our faith journey that if we encounter them without taking the time to prepare, we risk not grasping the fullness of God's love and grace. Our hearts, minds, and, yes, even our bodies need a time of preparation to lead us joyously to the feast, reluctantly to Gethsemane, solemnly to the cross, and jubilantly to the empty tomb. To participate in the fast during Lent, begin with Ash Wednesday on Day 1, and your journey will end on Easter.

However, you may use any 40-day period to begin this journey of self-examination that will help you focus unmistakably on Jesus. If you are fasting in the autumn season I suggest starting your journey on or near Yom Kippur, historically the Jewish Day of Atonement. This will typically conclude your fast a few weeks before the Thanksgiving and Christmas holidays.

Beginning with Day 1 on a Wednesday will mean the feast days fall on Sundays, which is fitting because Sundays are feast days in the Christian calendar. Bear in mind that while the fast lasts for 40 days, the experience takes place over 46 days because of the 6 feast days.

Embrace the feast days.

Feast days are a time for us to relax our fast and enjoy the extravagant grace of our Father. On these days especially it is good for us to spend time with friends and family, to enjoy the taste of food in a way we may never have before, and to give thanks to God who provides all we have. I'll say more about feasting in the next chapter.

As much as possible, eat food in its most natural state.

Have you ever eaten an entire artichoke? It is a favorite at our house. Artichokes are simple to prepare, just boil and enjoy with butter or olive oil. I find it remarkable that God created what is essentially a massive flower to be eaten as a delicacy; every petal when peeled back is an enjoyable sample of the indulgence to come. As you scrape your teeth over the individual petals, the anticipation builds until all are gone and you are left with God's greatest gift of the garden: the artichoke heart. I think of it as nature's filet mignon. And I imagine the artichoke as the food being enjoyed by the psalmist when he wrote:

> Taste of His goodness; see how wonderful the Eternal One
> truly is.
> Anyone who puts trust in Him will be blessed *and*
> *comforted.*"[1]

When my faith is soaring, my heart is content and I find great joy in small things: the bold flavors of African coffee, a piece of toast with apple butter, blue cheese on a simple salad, the complexities of sweet and salty in fresh sashimi. Maybe our enjoyment of the simple things in life has been lost because we so rarely eat the food God created for us.

In the United States, at least, what we often call food is actually processed far from its original state. Some products evidence more thought in the packaging than in the entrée itself. Is it possible we have lost a true sense of taste? Has our high-sodium fast-food diet warped our palettes? The artificial flavors created in laboratories certainly have the capacity to corrupt our senses so that we no longer know how to taste God's grace and goodness in what we eat.

Take your time shopping, looking over your food and appreciating its nourishment and beauty. Opt to put natural convenience foods (like fruit) in arms' reach to keep your diet rich in vitamins and minerals and eat as much fresh, ripe food as possible.

Approach this fast with a humble spirit.

Ask for humility, and be ready to receive. There is nothing more annoying than making a long trip with a driver who won't take directions, or working on a project with a know-it-all. You don't want to be *that* person on this sacred trek. In the same way, there is nothing more refreshing than a person of great intelligence who demonstrates his or her knowledge with love and grace, never seeking to make anyone feel unintelligent. Do you have moments when you bask in the joy of being correct? Ask God to transform your character in ways that lead you to be a person of humble strength, like Jesus. Paul reminds us of this potent truth:

> If you find any comfort from being in the Anointed, if His love brings you some encouragement, if you experience true companionship with the Spirit, if His tenderness and mercy fill your heart; *then, brothers and sisters, here is one thing that would* complete my joy—come together as one in mind and spirit and purpose, sharing in the same love. Don't let selfishness and prideful agendas take over. Embrace true humility, and lift your heads to extend love to

33

others. Get beyond yourselves and protecting your own interests; *be sincere*, and secure your neighbors' interests first.

In other words, adopt the mind-set of Jesus the Anointed. *Live with His attitude in your hearts.*[2]

Jesus talks about people who are fasting who go around looking pale and weak. If we do this, we are fasting for other people, not God. This journey is not about impressing anyone. As we look down this road, let us seek the Lord in a new way. May we set aside self-centered pursuits, may we grow spiritually and be changed. That is something worth pursuing. Jesus said it best:

> **Jesus:** And when you fast, do not look miserable as *the actors and* hypocrites do when they are fasting—*they walk around town putting on airs about their suffering and weakness, complaining about how hungry they are.* So everyone will know they are fasting, they don't wash or anoint themselves with oil, *pink their cheeks, or wear comfortable shoes. Those who show off their piety,* they have already received their reward.[3]

Realize that there may be many reasons to fast.

I do not fast in order to lose weight. But I know I weigh more than I should because I eat more calories than I need. Of course, my tendency is to add some excuse to explain away the weight. "My job is stressful, travel is hard, my metabolism changed quickly . . ." But in reality it comes back to the simple truth that I eat more than I need. A fast such as this is likely to bring my caloric intake down, which will result in a reasonable loss of weight. While the primary benefits of this experience are spiritual, don't be surprised to see physical benefits as well.

People fast from many different things, in many different ways, and for many different reasons. I would like you to avoid trying to sum up the reasoning for your fast with any singular purpose. It is too limiting in regard to the many things God will teach you on this journey. Would you like to develop a more intimate prayer life?

Yes. Would you like to develop a healthier and simpler diet that will sustain you long after this fast? Yes. Do you want to identify with the poor and become increasingly generous? Yes. Would you like to abandon patterns of addictive and selfish behavior? Yes. If you are like me and you weigh more than you should, would you like to lose weight? Yes. All of this is spiritual, and not one of these desired outcomes is unacceptable. In fact, I pray that you experience all of them.

We in the church have a nasty habit of trying to divorce the physical world from the spiritual world. Any attempt to act as if what God created (matter) is something that is not spiritual is not just a mistake, it is a heresy known as Gnosticism. So hear me clearly: my addiction to fresh tortilla chips and homemade salsa (impossible for me to resist) is a spiritual issue. The extra weight I carry with me is a spiritual issue, and it is never more painfully obvious than when I visit brothers and sisters living in extreme poverty. I have felt the gentle and loving rebuke of the Holy Spirit as I held an underweight child. I have too much, and she does not have enough. It is a painful realization, not only because it exposes my selfishness but also because it is clear to me that my sin is evident to everyone present. Sharing is at the heart of true Christianity.

Find a community.

It's true, Jesus fasted alone. He withdrew into the mountains in a desert of Jericho for 40 days. And there will certainly be times we desire solitude to read, pray, and rest. This will be a season of reflection. However, if we allow ourselves to become isolated, if we completely withdraw, the journey will be even more challenging, mainly because you (and I) are not Jesus. We tend to experience our greatest failures when we are alone. Forty days without fellowship and encouragement would be very hard. Find a group of friends and embark on this fast together. Pray for one another, support one another. Be honest about the struggles and failures.

Come around one another and say, "That's okay, we'll start again tomorrow." As Paul said,

> Shoulder each other's burdens, and then you will live as the law of the Anointed teaches us. Don't *take this opportunity to* think you are better than those who slip because you aren't; then you *become the fool and* deceive even yourself. Examine your own works so that if you are proud, it will be because of your own accomplishments and not someone else's. Each person has his or her own burden to bear *and story to write.*[4]

Ask your family if they are willing to join you on this fast.

One of the most important ways we can extend the positive impact of this journey is to include our families. Having said that, doctors advise against fasting for growing children (nursing or pregnant women also should not fast).

However, children can participate meaningfully in a number of ways. Following are practices that helped my children feel included:

- Allow your children to join the fast during certain meals or certain days. A meal of rice and beans once a week, for example, is not likely to do physical harm to your children.
- Ask your child to set the table and lead prayers for a child you sponsor or in response to one of the prayer requests that appear in the daily readings.
- Ask your children to incorporate a food staple like rice into their daily diet as a way to connect with children who rely on rice.
- Ask your children if they would be willing to fast in other ways, for example, limiting their TV, video game, or computer time.

Be creative. It is important not to force anything on your children, and even if they agree to a particular practice, show them grace if they falter. This isn't about adhering perfectly to a set of rules. It is about engaging a set of practices that bring us closer to God and each other.

Ask your church or small group to join you on this fast.

A wonderful way to participate in this fast is with your church and small group communities. You'll find the fast is easier if others are doing it with you, and you'll have the benefit of sharing and comparing experiences. Inevitably you will grow closer as brothers and sisters in Christ as you walk this road together. If nothing else, ask a friend to join you. A six-session DVD is available. Individuals can certainly benefit from this DVD, but it was created with groups and churches in mind. At the end of this book you'll find a DVD guide. For additional support, including videos, opportunities to connect with others doing the fast, and resources for doing *A Place at the Table* church series, see www.ChrisSeay.net.

Acknowledge your desires.

We are humans; we have desires. We have cravings. It is not that we shouldn't have them or should feel guilty when we do. We are not engaging in a form of punishment, penance, or body discipline; this is a search for clarity. Historically many have fasted as a means of suppressing desire (specifically, sexual desire). It is true that reducing your calorie intake to the lowest possible amount will curb even the most natural physical desires. Our goal during these 40 days, however, is not to suppress all our desires. Our goal is that our desires no longer drive our lives. When we make the choice to limit food choices, cravings will unleash for everything from chocolate to pickled jalapenos, rib-eye steaks to mozzarella, and that's just food. Our self-control will be put to the test when it comes to any number of desires. These desires may be healthy, destructive, or very revealing. You may desire quiet, a sexual connection with your spouse, diversions of all kinds; you may desire to kneel and pray, to connect with an old friend, or to go on a spontaneous road trip. Heighten your awareness of these desires and seek wisdom and discernment about how to respond. The desires that emerge from this fast will tell us a lot about ourselves: psychological weaknesses, character flaws, or things we desperately want but didn't know we wanted.

Consider doing a daily prayer walk.

Take time to walk one to two miles each day and pray for those in need. If we take 40 days to connect with the poor by eating what they eat, and if we join with the rest of the world that walks for miles to get to clean water, our bodies, minds, and spirits will be transformed. Simply take a walk around the block in the morning or at night, or spend some time on a treadmill.

Remember: this fast is between you and God.

Don't emulate anyone else or compare yourself. Don't expect that God will change you like He changes someone else. There is no one else on the planet quite like you. No one knows your inner thoughts, strengths, and potential like the One who created you. The Holy Spirit has a unique way of speaking to us when we stop long enough to truly listen. In fact, some of us may find gifts we never anticipated. You may find you are a poet, or a painter, or a songwriter, or have the gift of encouragement or teaching. Prepare for the unexpected. God may speak to you about lifestyle choices, your finances, the way you care for your body, or habits both good and bad.

Drink lots of water.

Our body is 60 to 75 percent water, so we need a tremendous amount of clean water to function at our best. Our bodies often mistake signals of thirst for hunger.

I am aware that I take clean water for granted. It flows directly into my house without my giving it a second thought. At no time in my life have I had to search or travel long distances to find water, as most of the world does. We live in a time when every fifteen seconds a child dies because they do not have access to clean water. Even to access dirty water, some people travel over 1 ½ miles (2.5 kilometers) a day to carry home a 50-pound container.

As you change your eating patterns during this fast, you can also take the opportunity to identify with the thirsty. Drink a lot of water. Look up the recommended amount for your body weight, take it in, and be grateful that you can. Share water and the conversation of the water crisis with others. It would be up to you if you added in any amounts of coffee, tea, or natural juices into your fast. In addition, during these 40 days, if you do a daily prayer walk, remember to pray for the water crisis and for ways to bring clean water to so many in need.

You can do this! Remember that.

Yes, some days are going to be difficult. As we take in fewer calories than our body has grown accustomed to, fear emerges as if our body is screaming for security. We will find excuses to stop fasting, but if we hang in there, God will use this fast for tremendous good. It is hard, but not impossible.

As we step into the wilderness, we will have to face many fears. The world's economy drives people by fear. God's way is to bring people comfort in grace and love. May we lay down our desires and seek the heart of God. When we begin to panic, when discomfort surfaces, may we turn to our Savior. May He use this time to start and complete wholeness in our mind, body, and spirit. May we get a glimpse into who we are in His eyes and what we can be as the church bride. Be courageous, step out in faith, lay yourself down for 40 days, and see what rises in your life. If Jesus chose to spend 40 days in a dry, arid desert to seek His Father and pray, surely we will be changed if we follow in His footsteps. God bless this time.

4

Fasting and Feasting

Embracing the Rhythm of the Kingdom

> Fasting expands our ideas of "feasting" on Christ.
> —Jan Johnson, *Fasting and Simplicity*

*C*larity. This is what I pray for all of us: moments of pause and visions of truth along the way.

Do you ever catch a glimpse of yourself in motion and at least for a second realize how frantic your pace is, how rarely you stop to rest, reflect, and listen?

> Be still, *be calm, see*, and understand I am the True God.
> I am honored among all the nations.
> I am honored over all the earth.[1]

Take a minute to gain an awareness of your breath. Do you have any compulsive behaviors? Twitching? Tapping? Checking your phone?

41

I have observed that frenetic people dine in a way that is hurried, distracted, and apathetic about the things that matter most. I have also observed that people who eat intentionally, taking time to savor flavors and engage the people around them, realize they are nourishing both their bodies and souls. This posture overflows into other areas of their lives, and they seem to live from a spring of wisdom and peace. Which came first, you wonder: the frenetic life or the unfortunate table manners? Thankfulness for the meal or a generous spirit? Hard to say, but it seems our conduct around the table is more than just an indicator that something in our life has gone awry; it is an all-out warning that we need to make some changes, to check our priorities. That's where we are headed. We are taking time to dial back our internal metronome. As we slow things down, we will begin to see things we never have before.

Years ago I made a pilgrimage to Kolkata, in many ways the epicenter of global poverty and the home of Mother Teresa. I was struggling to discern the right response for me personally to the desperate needs faced by so many brothers and sisters across the globe. I believed that somehow the wisdom from a radically loving believer like Mother Teresa, who had recently passed away, would guide me toward the answers I was seeking. I thought this twentieth-century hero of the poor must be the right person to guide me out of patterns of consumption and materialism. I never expected the answer I received. During the long flight from America I read a book that revealed Mother Teresa's profound struggle not only with caring for the poor but also, more surprisingly, with her doubt. Mother Teresa struggled to believe God truly loved her. In great candor she acknowledged to her spiritual director, "Jesus has a very special love for you. As for me, the silence and the emptiness is so great that I look and do not see, listen and do not hear."[2]

Teresa fasted and cared for the poor because so many of us in the West were unwilling. She lived a life of fasting but felt the painful absence of feasting. The reason Christians have historically taken a break from their fast on Sundays, as we do during Lent, is because we all need a day to focus entirely on the love of Jesus and the many blessings we enjoy that make that love so evident. I believe Teresa became so focused on her call to share the love of Jesus with the poor that she forgot to take time each week to bask in that love herself. For more than fifty years she could see clearly the love of Jesus for others but said she did not feel the love and presence of God for herself even once.

I implore you during this season not only to fast and identify with the poor but also to plan some parties, eat good food, and celebrate the love of Jesus well. Every Sunday for believers in Christ is to be a taste of our greatest day in the Christian calendar: Easter.

It became clear to me in Kolkata that I needed to loose the chains of materialism and give more generously than ever before, but I was also called to live a life of joy, not one of constant sorrow. Fasting alone is not a biblical response to poverty. Jesus said, "Guests at the wedding can't fast when the bridegroom is with them. It would be wrong to do anything but feast."[3] Our day of worship is a day to be present with the bridegroom. May we take six days of each week to identify with the poor and suffering as well as a day to rest in the loving and powerful arms of our risen Lord. Do not forsake him. Embrace the feast. Embrace the rhythm of the kingdom.

My problem, and possibly yours as well, is not that I spend too much time fasting or too much time feasting. My problem is that often I do neither. I simply consume my food. So as we embark on 40 days of fasting, it is important to take Sundays—the day when we focus on the groom (Jesus)—to break from fasting and embrace the feast. Here are a few suggestions to incorporate into your table life during this season as a means to guide you on the right path.

- **Put away your phone.** It is a distraction from the blessing of the food and the people before you. I have to place my phone in another room to keep my mind focused.
- **Observe natural colors.** Food is art. Soak in the natural beauty of the food, the table setting, and the people you are with from the start.
- **Savor flavors.** Take time to enjoy that unique meal. No other meal will be exactly the same.

- **Smell before you eat.** Inhale the fragrances, which will awaken your sense of taste.
- **Learn the art of great conversation.** Ask good questions, point out qualities in the food, and tell stories from your day that will edify others around the table.
- **Establish rituals.** Develop your own unique rituals. In my home, we collect all of the photos friends send to us as Christmas cards in a special prayer box, and every night we take out one photo and pray for that family.
- **Remember the poor.** Find creative ways to remember those in need, in prayer and in gifts.

The choices are not merely to sell all you have to serve the poor or to keep living in a way that maintains the status quo. I have found both of these to be faulty models. The third path is filled with self-denial, immense celebrations, laughter, great food, and a clear conscience. We need to take time to connect with the poor, resist our unceasing cravings, and pray. But we also need to gather with friends and family, share in God's good provision, eat delicious food, tell stories that encourage us all, and celebrate the risen Lord.

One of my greatest mentors in the faith is a man we know as St. Patrick. He shared many gifts but was known most for going back to the place where he was enslaved and sharing the love of Jesus in a way that was truly transforming. In his lifetime the Irish isles went from being the least Christian province to the most Christian province in the known world. Patrick was a man with a gift of prayer and a love for hospitality and creativity. One of the reasons we celebrate St. Patrick's Day the way we do is because hospitality and feasting were a really big deal for St. Patrick and the Celts. They invited everyone to celebrate the pleasures God had provided for them. They knew the blessing of the feast. In fact, in Celtic Christian communities, you would never find someone without a place to eat or sleep. Hospitality was a mandate for all who followed Christ. Can you imagine if our churches made feasting and hospitality a mandate? If we required everyone to open their homes as a demonstration of the kingdom, even disciplining those who failed to do so? According to the Scriptures, we are to show hospitality to all people, specifically immigrants:

> You must treat the outsider as one of your native-born people—as a full citizen—and you are to love him in the same way you love yourself; for *remember,* you were once strangers living in Egypt. I am the Eternal One, your God.[4]

But Celtic Christians didn't merely bring you in for bread and water and a roof over your head. These kinsmen and kinswomen considered it a blessing to serve the Lord and encounter Christ in a physical way. One of my favorite Celtic prayers echoes this sentiment:

> I saw a stranger yestereen,
> I put food in the eating place
> drink in the drinking place
> music in the listening place
> and in the sacred names of the Holy Trinity,
> he blessed my house,
> my cattle and my dear ones,
> and the lark sang her song often,
> often, often goes the Christ in a strangers guise,
> often, often, often goes the Christ in the strangers guise.[5]

The Celts took the words of Scripture very seriously, believing that in strangers we often encounter angels and even Jesus himself:

> Don't forget to extend your hospitality to all—even to strangers—for *as you know,* some have unknowingly shown kindness to heavenly messengers in this way.[6]

I have to admit, too often I fail to live fully into this beautiful gift of hospitality. It makes me wonder how many times I may have turned away Jesus in the form of a desperate immigrant or a homeless brother or sister. My wife, Lisa, and I have learned that when we practice hospitality well, we are at our best. The Celts knew how to welcome strangers. They played music. They feasted, they partied. They gathered their tribe to enjoy the blessings, to encounter Christ, to encounter angels, and make sure that all were included. I pray, I dream that we become a people who are known not because we have a huge steeple or beautiful stained glass or interesting buildings but because we are so hospitable, so celebratory, that we are constantly inviting others in and sharing Jesus.

If you choose a path that tries to connect with the least of these, to better understand people you haven't ever met, people you can share your extras with (because none of us will be going without), it is an act of courage. Maya Angelou says, "Without courage, you cannot practice any other virtue consistently."[7] I think she is exactly right. Fasting is not a virtue. You could do it for all the wrong reasons. You could do it to look pious and religious; you could do it to try to show off for your family and friends; you could do it because you are tired of dieting. The right reason to fast is because it facilitates a deeper relationship with God, and our hearts will be transformed, and likely along the way so too will our bodies, our family relationships, and our relationship to the poor.

Fasting is courageous. And when we have the courage to live a life that is not devoted to our own desires, we will practice the virtues of faith, hope, and love more consistently. Our families and the world do not need more religious rituals—they desperately need the radical love and generosity that this specific religious ritual can produce if we give our hearts to it. Imagine with me a world transformed by this kind of love, and let it begin today.

Prayer

Lord, would You shift something in our hearts and help us to become more like you? We open our hearts to you, that You would shape us into people of radical hospitality, people who give and share and offer food and drink and music and laughter and dance and all the hope of Jesus in our homes.

God, bless our homes as welcoming places. Build into our houses hope and hospitality. Be among us, not only in our church buildings but also in our homes. We commit our homes to You, that these would be beachheads, places of light and refuge, bright places in our neighborhoods that keep them from rotting and decaying. God, thank You for including us in Your story. Teach us to live fully into Your continual development of love and grace in the name of the Father, the Son, and the Holy Spirit. Amen.

Daily Readings

It behooves us then, to humble ourselves before the offended power, to confess our national sins, and to pray for clemency and forgiveness.

—Abraham Lincoln, proclaiming a National
Fast Day during the Civil War

God speaks in so many unique ways—through nature, friends, mentors, teachers, pastors, musicians, animals, popular culture, family, books, silence, and sometimes chaos. But I have learned that the voice of God becomes difficult to hear when I am not immersed in the Scriptures. My role in this book is to invite you not only to read the Scriptures each day but also to truly live inside the biblical narrative. Stories like the Exodus are recorded in Scripture as more than mere history. It is a gift to understand some of the historical facts of the Hebrew people. But the account we are given of the Exodus is much more than historical; it is personal and inspirational. This narrative is at the heart of the Pentateuch because it is a story that binds us all together. We are all slaves to something. As Bob Dylan says, "You're gonna have to serve somebody."

In these daily readings we will walk through two stories: the story of the Exodus and the story of Jesus's final days and His death and resurrection. But these two stories are really one story; they belong to one narrative. Jesus came to complete the final exodus; He completes our journey home through His sacrificial death and victorious resurrection. In fact, when Jesus visits with Moses and Elijah on the Mount of Transfiguration, they speak of Jesus's final exodus.

The problems we are contemplating on this journey—global poverty, consumerism, compulsions, addictions, and so on—will not be solved merely by giving the problems greater attention. The answers are found in Jesus. Our goal is to focus our affection and attention on Jesus and experience a miraculous exodus that can come only by His hand. Together we will focus on the journey of God's people to find freedom through a physical exodus in the wilderness. At the same time we will engage in a spiritual exodus through the work of Jesus our Liberating King.

These readings were written as I fasted in 2011, so you will hear clearly my frustration, my struggles with my own sin, and my longing to experience God's transforming love as the truest mark of this spiritual and physical exercise. The following daily readings will help us to engage God's story; examine our lives in the context of the Scriptures; acknowledge the sins and struggles that are being exposed as we lay down our selfish desires; and pray for our brothers and sisters struggling in abject poverty as well as find ways to share our resources with them.

I cannot tell you the best time of day to engage in the readings. Often it is best for us to focus our heart's attention in the morning, but if you have young children, a challenging work schedule, or find that you don't function at full capacity until noon, do these daily devotions in the evening. In those cases, it might be worthwhile to refresh your focus in the morning by choosing to pray in response to one of the prayer requests that appear in the daily readings. My hope is that the names of the people in these requests will be ringing in your ears throughout the day and that hundreds and thousands of prayers will be lifted for them.

I encountered God on this journey and it changed me. I pray nothing less for you.

Day 1

Brothers and sisters,

As we set out on this journey, we share many common fears of failure and discomfort. We carry with us gnawing suspicions that when we strip away the many comforts of our dietary pleasures, we may not like what we see in ourselves. We also share a tendency to want to control this journey. If you have fasted or attempted a fast before, or if you are already aware of food or things you rely on for comfort, you may be harboring plans for special snacks, diversions, old habits, online addictions, or excessive faith in your own willpower. It makes sense; you have totally taken control of this area in your life, and walking into vulnerability can stir up fears of famine in us. John Steinbeck says, "A journey is like a marriage. The certain way to be wrong is to think that you can control it."

In time it will become painfully clear that we are not the pilots of this ship. Submission to our King is the only way forward.

Have you ever lost your child, even for a moment, while walking through the aisles of a grocery store? What happened? I speak from experience when I say the feeling goes far beyond distress and panic. Literally every fiber of my being contracts with complete focus on one task: FIND MY CHILD! If it means running through a wall, so be it.

My son Solomon has a wandering spirit and has caused me this kind of agony more than once. We learned when Solomon was three that he had a habit of waking up with the sun and secretly venturing out our back door and around our urban neighborhood in his pajamas. One Saturday morning a neighbor knocked on our door after Solomon quietly snuck back into the house before we woke. This neighbor had spotted him blocks away from our house, enjoying his clandestine morning walk, and thought it might be time for the parents to be alerted to his behavior. When I heard what he had been up to, I froze in fear of the unforeseen danger he could have faced and what I would have done if I had awoken to find him missing.

So imagine the violent rebellion of the Israelites when Pharaoh gave this decree:

In response *to the rapid growth in the Hebrew population,* Pharaoh issued a command to his people.

Pharaoh: Every boy who is born *to the Hebrews* must be thrown into the Nile, and every girl is to be left alive.[1]

Surely, Hebrew parents set the palace of Pharaoh ablaze and fought for their newborn sons to the death, right? No, they handed their babies over to be plunged into the crocodile-infested Nile River. Unbelievable. How could parents ignore their most basic primal instinct to protect their children?

Slavery. They were living in submission to an unforgiving master. Though Pharaoh abused and mistreated them, they obeyed him and sought to please him.

Slavery and her evil sister addiction will take everything you have and come back for more. Look at your own addictions and besetting sins. Do they lead you to illogical thinking, shameful mistakes, and broken relationships? Walter Brueggemann says the key to making an exodus is in understanding this: "You owe Pharaoh nothing. You are free."[2] You don't have to mindlessly obey the mad impulses that master you. You are free indeed.

This is a realization that can come only after we acknowledge that we are living as slaves. The next step is battling the inevitable paralysis that comes when we imagine what freedom might look like. Over the weeks to come, pray you can address your own Pharaohs, the things/people/cravings that own you. They may be pornographies of sexuality, gluttony, greed, consumerism, compulsive behaviors, or sinful habits. But the truth is they do not own us and we owe them nothing. Like Pharaoh of Egypt, our cruel masters seek to take our lives and destroy our children.

In Egypt, the Israelites spent their days tirelessly making bricks for a brutal dictator while handing their babies over to certain death. All of them, that is, except for one woman:

> *One day* a man and woman—both from the tribe of Levi—married. She became pregnant and gave birth to a son. When she saw that her son was *healthy and* beautiful, *she feared for his safety;* so she kept him hidden from view for three whole months.
>
> When she could no longer keep him hidden away, she took a basket made of reeds, sealed it with tar and pitch, and placed her baby boy in it. Then she wedged the basket among the reeds along the edge of the Nile River.
>
> *All the while,* the child's sister watched from a distance to see what might happen to her baby brother.
>
> *Later on* Pharaoh's daughter came down to bathe in the river while her young attendants walked along the bank *nearby.* Pharaoh's daughter noticed the basket *wedged* among the reeds *and wondered what it might contain.* So she instructed her maid to bring it to her. When Pharaoh's daughter opened the basket, she found the baby boy. He was crying, and her heart melted with compassion.
>
> **Pharaoh's Daughter:** This is a Hebrew child.
>
> **Child's Sister** *(coming out of her hiding place)*: Would you like me to find a Hebrew woman to nurse the child for you?
>
> **Pharaoh's Daughter:** All right. *Go find a nurse.*
>
> So the baby's sister went and fetched his mother. *The boy's mother approached Pharaoh's daughter.*[3]

Like the mother of Moses, you and I have a way out, but it will require creativity, obedience, and boldness beyond anything we have known before. It will call for a refusal to bow to destructive desires. How will you stand up to your Pharaohs on this journey? Has fear been the deterrent from complete restoration? Does facing an addiction seem like more than you can handle? Our time has come.

Prayer

God, give us the clarity to battle our Pharaohs and bring a new sense of freedom to this generation and the next. We thank You for the beauty of Your sacred and divine story that declares to us clearly that we are a people freed from a cruel master. We have been bought by one who came to redeem and free us. He called us to live as we are intended to live: in grace and hope. Lord, may we find that new freedom as we declare Your lordship in our lives. You are our one true master.

IRENE IN UGANDA

Irene lives with her parents, who find work as part-time common laborers, in Uganda, East Africa. At home she helps out by carrying water and firewood. Irene enjoys singing, telling stories, and jumping rope with her friends. In her rural village, lack of education and opportunities result in early pregnancies and ongoing poverty. Corn, beans, and cassava are staple foods, but malnutrition is common. The nearest medical center is a one-hour walk away. Pray that Irene will grow up protected from serious illnesses like malaria and HIV, and that her community will have clean water soon. Pray that God will instill in Irene a deep sense of her value to Him.

Day 2

If this journey is to transform us, it will require us to better understand a reality we tend to ignore personally, historically, and as a present crisis: slavery. It is not a word that evokes positive feelings. Whether you live in the North, South, Southwest, or Midwest you likely feel some sense of anguish, grief, and shame about the history of slavery in the United States. Globally, twenty-seven million people still live in slavery. Half of these slaves are children. This is something I know in my head, but it is difficult to translate in my heart. When I look at the shelves of chocolate in my local convenience store, I know that much of the cacao farmed across the globe comes from children who are forced into labor due to unjust debt. But I ignore it.

In the same way, I ignore many facts in my own life that point to one irrefutable conclusion: I am a slave. I am a slave to my job, my fears, my cravings, my beloved possessions, my technological gadgets, my dreams for the future, and my sense of well-being that comes from the approval of other people. I need an exodus. We all do.

Do you feel stuck in a dead-end job? You need an exodus. Have you lost your passion for life and for God? You need an exodus. Has the American way of life left you trapped by debt and surrounded by possessions that you do not actually need? Time for an exodus.

The good news is you have taken a courageous step toward freedom. Courage is essential for this journey. The bad news is that each brave step in our emancipation journey will likely bring challenges while leading us away from our usual comforts.

The exodus of God's children began when God spoke to Moses. I am confident that along this path God will speak to us as well. In Exodus 3 we hear this matchless story:

When the Eternal One saw Moses approach *the burning bush* to observe it *more closely,* He called out to him from within the bush.

Eternal One: Moses! Moses!

Moses: I'm right here.

Eternal One: Don't come any closer. Take off your sandals *and stand barefoot on the ground in My presence,* for this ground is holy ground. I am the True God, *the God* of your father, the God of Abraham, Isaac, and Jacob.

A feeling of dread and awe rushed over Moses; he hid his face because he was afraid he might catch a glimpse of the True God.

Eternal One: I have seen how My people in Egypt are being mistreated. I have heard their groaning when the slave drivers torment and harass them; for I know well their suffering. I have come to rescue them from the oppression of the Egyptians, to lead them from that land *where they are slaves and* to give them a good land—a wide, open space flowing with milk and honey. The land is currently inhabited by Canaanites, Hittites, Amorites, Perizzites, Hivites, and Jebusites. The plea of Israel's children has come before Me, and I have observed the cruel treatment they have suffered by Egyptian hands. So go. I'm sending you *back to Egypt as My messenger* to the Pharaoh. *I want you to gather My people*—the children of Israel—and bring them out of Egypt.

Moses *(to God)*: Who am I to confront Pharaoh and lead Israel's children out of Egypt?

Eternal One: *Do not fear, Moses.* I will be with you *every step of the way,* and this will be the sign to you that I am the One who has sent you: after you have led them out of Egypt, you will return to this mountain and worship God.[4]

Moses, like you and me, was afraid. His fears seemed to come back often. But the beauty of the exodus is found in the ways he embraced faith over fear. This too is our journey. Are you aware of the chains that bind you? Do you believe that God sees you in the midst of your suffering and slavery? Do you believe He has made a provision for your liberation?

Prayer

God, we thank You for being near in a world filled with selfish ambition, where too often our tendency is to turn inward and contemplate our own desires despite the suffering that surrounds us. We are grateful that this 40-day journey calls us deeper into a story that reminds and informs us of the truth of who we really are, and that You came into this world to reveal Yourself in love and to lead us in turning outward and sharing that love.

We live surrounded by a wealth that defies the imagination of our poorer brothers and sisters, yet we live with the fear that we will never have enough. May we hear Your voice as Moses heard You speak long ago and respond in obedience, sharing in radical ways.

Expand our hearts, Lord, that we may learn to truly love. Give us ears to hear You in a new way through the Scriptures and to discover the path of our own exodus. Give us the patience required to learn and the faith to know that You are all that we need. Amen.

RUTH IN HAITI

Ruth lives with her mother and six brothers and sisters in a coastal community near Port-au-Prince. She carries water and helps with gardening and caring for animals. Her mother sells fruits and vegetables part-time at the market. Fish, plantains, and rice are part of Ruth's common diet, but in her large family, there is often not enough food for everyone to eat. There is no good water supply or proper sanitation, so intestinal disease is common. Pray for Ruth and the rest of her siblings, that they will work together to help their mother and will be a strong family who pulls together in difficulty. Pray that they will know God's love and presence in their lives.

Day 3

Reading the stories of God's rescuing work throughout the Scriptures is inspiring. It gives us a new way to see our problems and a hope that we will experience deliverance. One of the major obstacles to deliverance, however, is our failure to see the ways that God can use us. We tend to elevate the great heroes of our faith like Moses, David, Solomon, or Paul. But the truth is they may not have been any more gifted than any of us. In fact, you could easily make a case they were less talented, less articulate, or less intelligent. They possessed flaws in their character and were stubborn to a fault.

Honestly, if we look at young Moses, we can see that he had done nothing to distinguish himself. He was an outsider living like an insider only because he was found floating in a river and a young princess did not have the heart to drown him as was required by law. He lived in Pharaoh's house, ate his food, and enjoyed his wealth, but it's quite possible he was never seen as a full-fledged member of their family. He struggled to speak, and he would never feel fully at home among his people or among Egyptian royalty. So why would God use this young man?

What Moses had going for him was his upbringing amidst power and wealth (Pharaoh) and a heart that could be moved by God toward justice. We share these traits with our brother Moses. We live among the wealthiest people on the planet and are also on a journey into the wilderness, where we seek to encounter God. Is it possible that we, like Moses, will be so changed by our encounter with God that we will use our access to the legislative process and power to see justice on earth? Don't misunderstand me: seeking power as its own reward is literally a fool's errand. But using the considerable power every Westerner already enjoys for the sake of the poor is both righteous and life-changing—for us and for the poor.

Moses found the mission he was made for; are you willing to discover yours? When we begin to take courageous steps to end poverty, modern-day slavery, and the water crisis, our actions easily multiply because of our influence on the people in our lives. When entire churches begin to feel a truly familial connection with the least of these, the world will never be the same.

Are you tired? Frustrated by failures or meaningless tasks? You might think it is because you are doing too much, but what if it is because you are busy doing all the wrong things? Hear the words of Jesus in Matthew 11:

Jesus: Come to Me, all who are weary and burdened, and I will give you rest. Put My yoke upon your shoulders—*it might appear heavy at first, but it is perfectly fitted to your curves.* Learn from Me, for I am gentle and humble of heart. *When you are yoked to Me,* your weary souls will find rest. For My yoke is easy, and My burden is light.[5]

Jesus says He will give us rest by putting a yoke around our neck. Sounds like work, right? It is, but it is the work we are made to do. Join me in praying that you will fully discover that mission and calling for your life. When you do, it will be a thing of beauty.

Prayer

God, we are so thankful that You use all things to draw us near to You. Regardless of who we are, what we wear, who we know, what we drive, You meet us. You come to us in the slums as well as the heights. You give us opportunities to be a part of Your kingdom here on earth. We long for heaven. Give us a foretaste of Your love, grace, and beauty as we seek to live as family with those suffering near and far. We thank You that You can use us in

the same ways You have used the great heroes of the Bible. Lead
us on that path, Lord. Amen.

ANAND IN INDIA

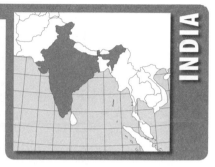

Anand is a full-time missionary to the prisons in Kerala, a state in southern India. Although he has spent much of his time ministering to inmates, he wants to be a missionary to his neighbors too. Anand lives in a predominantly Hindu village. He set out to develop friendships with the people in the neighborhood, but they knew he was a Christian and would have nothing to do with him. His village had one problem that was shared by Christian and Hindu alike—there was never enough water. Anand found out about Living Water International through a local pastor and was able to make arrangements for a team to come and drill a well. At the well dedication ceremony, a councilwoman, a Hindu, said, "They have come to do this for us because of the love of Jesus." The well stands at the center of the neighborhood, near Anand's home, and is pumped almost constantly. "The neighborhood is a community now," Anand tells us. Pray for water ministries to continue building bridges into communities that seem unreachable.

Day 4

To be honest, this fourth day of Lent is hard for me. The combination of head-splitting predicaments, pressing responsibilities, and the fact that there are thirty-six more days of caffeine headaches ahead in this fast makes me feel doubtful that I will be able to continue.

The voice of doubt is one we all have to battle. Have you battled that fear today? I have. But I find hope when I imagine the insecurity of Moses. Warring on a daily basis with the diffidence of being adopted into a family where he clearly did not belong, I imagine Moses was afraid to identify completely with his native people and yet was fully aware that his status in the royal family was dubious. As if that weren't enough, Moses could hardly complete a sentence without tripping over his own tongue. He certainly must have wondered (as King George VI did in the movie *The King's Speech*) which came first: the stutter or the insecurity?

Even as Moses experiences a supernatural call in the form of a real God encounter, his doubts rise to the surface:

Moses: What if they don't trust me? What if they don't listen to a single word I say? They are *more likely* to reply: "The Eternal has not revealed Himself to you."

The Eternal One answered Moses.

Eternal One: What do you have in your hand?

Moses: My *shepherd's* staff.

Eternal One: Throw your staff down on the ground.

So Moses threw the staff on the ground, and it was transformed into a snake. Moses quickly jumped back *in fear.*

Eternal One: Reach out and grab it by the tail.

Despite his natural fears, Moses reached out and grabbed the snake; and as he held it, it changed back into a shepherd's staff.

Eternal One: This *sign* is so the people will believe that I, the God of their fathers—Abraham, Isaac, and Jacob—has revealed Himself to you.
     Now *for the second sign.* Put your hand *on your chest* inside your shirt.

Moses did as the Eternal instructed; and when he pulled his hand out, his hand was covered with some disease *that made it look* as white as snow.

Eternal One: Put your hand back inside your clothes.

Moses again did as He instructed, and when he removed his hand from his shirt, it returned *to normal* like the rest of his skin.

Eternal One: If they refuse to believe you, and are not persuaded after *you perform* the first sign, perhaps they will be after the second sign. But if they refuse to believe you and are not persuaded after *you perform* the first two signs, then *here is a third sign:* Take some water from the Nile and pour it out onto the ground. The water you take from the Nile will become blood on the ground.

Moses: Please, Lord, *I am not a talented speaker.* I have never been good with words. I wasn't when I was younger and I haven't gotten any better since You revealed Yourself to me. I stutter and stammer. My words get all twisted.

Eternal One: Who is it that gives a person a mouth? Who determines whether one person speaks and another doesn't? Why is it that one person hears and another doesn't? And why can one person see and another doesn't? Isn't it *because of* Me, the Eternal? *You know it is.* Go now, and I will be there to give you the words to speak; I will tell you what to say.

Moses: Please, Lord, *I beg You to* send *Your message through* someone else, *anyone else.*

Then the Eternal became angry with Moses.

Eternal One: How about your brother—Aaron the Levite? I know he speaks eloquently. And look, he is already on his way to meet you. When he sees you, his heart will be delighted. I want you to talk to him and put the *right* words in his mouth. I will guide your mouth and his mouth and instruct you both on what you should do. He will address the people as your spokesman. He will serve as your mouth; and you will instruct him in what he is to say as if you were God to him.

Take this staff in your hand, and use it to perform the signs I have shown you.[6]

Moses's struggle with self-doubt reminds me of one of my all-time favorite singers, Nina Simone. She was the daughter of a black preacher in the South, and she may be one of the greatest jazz singer-songwriters who ever lived. Yet, not least because of racism and prejudice, she doubted herself terribly. Nina Simone could set a room ablaze with the sound of her voice and the passion of her words. Moses held up his arms and saw God part the sea before him. And still both were plagued by self-doubt and despair. Why should we be any better than either of them? But God also has a plan for us. He used Moses to lead his people out of Egypt, and Nina Simone to lead her people out of oppression and into a better day through her music and her work in the civil rights movement. God also intends to use each of us. May we pause today to reconnect with that truth and summon the courage to walk into another day by His grace.

Prayer

God, we realize that the day-to-day problems we face are so small and that our faith is often not what it should be. Moses and Nina struggled to feel assured, just as we often do. Instill in us the confidence of Your presence. Move us to a higher ground, and give us a better vantage point to see how we can join in Your work in the world near and far.

DR. CHARLES IN SIERRA LEONE

In 2007, Dr. Charles diagnosed more than fifty cases of cholera in a town in Sierra Leone. The town's health clinic had a broken-down hand pump behind their building, which was actually something of an improvement on the contaminated open wells spread out in the surrounding areas. Living Water was able to restore the clinic's broken pump and rehabilitate many of the open wells in the area and, in all of 2008, Dr. Charles didn't diagnose a single case of cholera. He's pretty sure the new wells have something to do with it. Pray for the millions of people suffering from water-borne illnesses.

FEAST DAY: Celebrating Well

Whether this is your first time participating in a fast of any kind or you practice this discipline regularly, fasting is not easy. If you're not struggling a bit, you are probably not really fasting. This kind of holy disruption of our routines forces us to contemplate our choices and see the sacredness in everything we do.

During a recent trip to Israel I intentionally visited the mountain that is thought to be the place where Jesus fasted for 40 days. As I sat on that mountain and prayed, a story came to mind, and it is one that I believe will be important and transforming for all of us on this journey. Sometime after His fast, Jesus returned to a mountainous area, but this time He was not alone.

Jesus left and went to the Sea of Galilee. He went up on a mountaintop and sat down. Crowds thronged to Him there, bringing the lame, *the maimed,* the blind, the crippled, the mute, and many other *sick and broken* people. They laid them at His feet, and He healed them. The people saw the mute speaking, the lame walking, *the maimed made whole,* the crippled dancing, and the blind seeing; and the people were amazed, and they praised the God of Israel.

Jesus *(to His disciples):* *We must take pity on* these people for they have touched My heart; they have been with Me for three days, and they don't have any food. I don't want to send them home this hungry—they might collapse on the way!

66

Disciples: We'll never find enough food for all these people, out here in the middle of nowhere!

Jesus: How much bread do you have?

Disciples: Seven *rounds of flatbread* and a few small fish.

He told the crowd to sit down. He took the bread and the fish, He gave thanks, and then He broke the bread and divided the fish. He gave the bread and fish to the disciples, the disciples distributed them to the people, and everyone ate and was satisfied. When everyone had eaten, the disciples picked up seven baskets of *crusts and* broken pieces *and crumbs*.

There were 4,000 men there, not to mention all the women and children. Then Jesus sent the crowd away. He got into His boat and went to Magadan.[7]

Jesus gathered with the crowd on the mountain, and no one had any food to eat. Interesting. Was this a spontaneous trip or were these people all so desperately poor that they had no food? As a child I was always taught that the crowd was a large group of people who happened to be remarkably forgetful. They went to follow Jesus without packing a lunch. But it dawned on me while sitting on the Mountain of Temptation in Jericho that the crowd may have assumed that this was a spiritual time reserved for teaching and fasting. Fasting is, and has always been, an important spiritual discipline, and many may have known that Jesus himself had recently taken 40 days to fast and pray. But Jesus was known for defying the stereotypes, and we know Jesus was not a fan of fasting for show. He received questions on more than one occasion about the reasons He or His disciples were often found feasting and dining with notorious sinners. They were known more for being a feasting people than a fasting people.

Imagine this: the crowd had gathered on what had become a three-day spiritual retreat, expecting to hear Jesus teach, and to fast and pray. Instead, Jesus broke this fast with a miracle that resulted in fish and bread for all, so much food that the leftovers have become a historic symbol of abundance. In the midst of the fast Jesus declared that it was time to celebrate. Many of us carry an image in our minds of a solemn and quiet picnic. I think not. If you were eating miraculous food with the Savior, how would you behave? This was a party! In the same way, I want to encourage you to take this Sunday, a day of worship, as a sacred feasting day. Historically this has been the pattern the church has followed during Lent—six days to fast and one to feast. If you do this well, it will be a beautiful day of worship and an important part of our fasting journey. Here are a few of my thoughts on how to do it well:

- **Gather with some friends and family.** Feasting days are days to be with people you love, both at church and at home.
- **Share with a friend something God is teaching you.** We need to celebrate the fact that we are growing in our relationship with the Lord.
- **Do not overeat.** Feasting is not synonymous with gluttony, and overeating will only make the upcoming days of your fast more difficult.
- **Avoid food triggers on feasting days.** Have a particular bond with chocolate, for instance? We are in the midst of a time when we are learning not to let our longings and desires become idols. If we are not careful, our days of feasting can become times that we will daydream about throughout the week. So it may be best to leave the chocolate alone.
- **Toast.** Lift a glass to those with whom you dine, and speak a blessing over each of them.
- **Pray.** This is a day to soak in your many blessings and devote a substantial amount of time to prayer. If you can, take one hour to walk and pray on feasting days.

Prayer

God, we thank You for the feasting table. It is a foretaste of heaven itself, and on this day of worship we pause from our fast to celebrate Your love and grace. Amen.

SIMONETTE IN HAITI

Simonette lives with her parents and three siblings in Port-au-Prince, Haiti. Her father works part-time at their church, and her mother stays at home. Simonette helps out at home by carrying water and washing clothes. She enjoys skipping rope with her friends and singing at church, where she receives help through Compassion International. The church is actively working to teach Simonette and her friends about daily health, cleanliness, and nutrition. Pray that Simonette will have new opportunities to learn and grow physically, mentally, and spiritually, and that she will have an open heart for memorizing Scripture and being a good example to the other students around her. Pray that her family will have enough to eat.

Day 5

We live in the most convenient of times. If you just sat for one moment and contemplated what processes it took to produce the book you are holding, the chair you are sitting on, what you are wearing or eating, you might be astounded at the hours of work that someone else has done on your behalf. I don't want to give convenience a bad rap. Ideally, we'd live in communities where we would all share of our trades, land, and harvest. What I am saying is that it may not be the best thing to be getting so much so often without having to put forth much of our own effort. We start to complain about wait times, service failures, and mechanical malfunctions that disrupt our continual input flow of "I get what I want when I want it." But growing accustomed to convenience isn't all that entitlement is about. It's also about believing it is our right to have "it" for whatever reason. We have done A, sacrificed B, and paid the price for C, so now we deserve D and its full benefits. "I give so much over here, it's okay if I take some extra for myself from over there." What's worse is the idea that we have become a people who aren't gifted with grace, but people who think we can earn it or somehow deserve it.

Jesus asks us to pursue the things that God values. To stretch out, to do Kingdom work, and not to worry—He will provide for our daily needs.

Jesus (then, to His disciples): This is why I keep telling you not to worry about anything in life—about what you'll eat, about how you'll clothe your body. Life is more than food, and the body is more than fancy clothes. Think about those crows flying over there: do they plant and harvest crops? Do they own silos or barns? *Look at them fly*. It looks like God is taking pretty good care of them, doesn't it? Remember

70

that you are more precious to God than birds! Which one of you can add a single hour to your life or 18 inches to your height by worrying really hard? If worry can't change anything, why do you do it so much?

Think about those beautiful wild lilies growing over there. They don't work up a sweat toiling for needs or wants—they don't worry about clothing. Yet the great King Solomon never had an outfit that was half as glorious as theirs!

Look at the grass growing over there. One day it's thriving in the fields. The next day it's being used as fuel. *If God takes such good care of such transient things,* how much more you can depend on God to care for you, weak in faith as you are. Don't reduce your life to the pursuit of food and drink; don't let your mind be filled with anxiety. People of the world who don't know God pursue these things, *but you have a Father caring for you,* a Father who knows all your needs.

*Since you don't need to worry—about security and safety, about food and clothing—*then pursue God's kingdom *first and foremost,* and these other things will come to you as well.[8]

These words were likely deeply convicting to those who heard Jesus utter them, but how much more so for each of us. We busy ourselves with worry not about daily sustenance but most often about status. We do not fear that we will not have enough to eat—for most of us this is a non-issue. But we worry and fret over having the right clothes, driving the right car, and living in the right part of town.

If entitlement is like a disease to a healthy spiritual life, then gratitude is the proven vaccine. What lengths are you willing to go to in order to integrate a grateful spirit into everything that you do? I love the way that G. K. Chesterton said it: "When we were children we were grateful to those who filled our stockings at Christmas time. Why are we not grateful to God for filling our stockings with legs?"[9]

The list of things that we take for granted seems unending: fresh-baked bread, crisp apples, the warm light through the window, the kind touch of a friend, joyous reunions, clean water, transportation, a vocation, family, friends . . . every breath is a gift.

The fact that our blood is constantly pumping through every artery in our body, and that God has made us to walk, run, speak, sing, and dance is a miracle. Do you think God becomes tired of hearing our thanks for these blessings? I doubt it; how could we ever say it enough? The psalmist seems to say it over and over again; maybe we should as well.

> *Let your heart overflow with* praise to the Eternal, for He
>   is good,
>   for His faithful love lasts forever.
> Praise the True God *who reigns* over all other gods,
>   for His faithful love lasts forever.
> Praise the Lord *who reigns* over all other lords,
>   for His faithful love lasts forever.
>
> To Him who alone does marvelous wonders,
>   for His faithful love lasts forever.
> Who created the heavens with skill *and artistry*,
>   for His faithful love lasts forever.
> Who laid out dry land over the waters,
>   for His faithful love lasts forever.
> Who made the great *heavenly* lights,
>   for His faithful love lasts forever.
> The sun to reign by day,
>   for His faithful love lasts forever.
> The moon and stars to reign by night,
>   for His faithful love lasts forever. [10]

Would you try an experiment with me today? On a single sheet of paper, will you write words of thanks? As you become aware of your blessings today, write them down. Some blessings are large and some might seem small. God has given you 86,400 seconds today—use as many of them as possible to say thanks.

Prayer

God, You have given us so much, and if we fail to express our thanks, we might come to believe that we deserve all of these blessings. They come from You as gifts. Would You give us grateful hearts that lead us down a path of generosity? We are grateful for the warmth of the sun, the lessons learned from hard work, the peace found in a good night's sleep, the rains that nourish the earth, the fantastical colors that charm our eyes, the tastes of delicacies both salty and sweet, and the unmatched fragrance of home. It all comes from You, God, as an extravagant display of Your love for us. Forgive us when we ignore it, and allow Your love to draw us near to You this day. Amen.

PEDRO IN BRAZIL

Pedro lives with his foster parents and sibling in eastern Brazil. Neither of his parents has a full-time job, but sometimes they both find work as day laborers. Pedro helps out at home, running errands and cleaning, and on a normal day might eat corn, beans, bananas, and chicken. For fun, Pedro enjoys soccer, playing with toy cars, and telling stories. He attends church activities and Bible class regularly and is a good student. Poor community sanitation leads to worms and parasite infections, asthma, and frequent illnesses among children in Pedro's community. Pray that Pedro and his family will feel God's presence in their lives and that God will move in a way that would remove his community's sanitation problem.

Day 6

I often watch the television show *House M.D.*, a weekly drama that is usually formulaic and predictable. But I can't get enough. In every episode a patient faces certain death if Dr. House is not able to make some sense out of their complex and often contradictory symptoms. Without an accurate diagnosis the result is death, and the path to an accurate diagnosis comes only from careful observation of the symptoms.

The same principle holds true if we seek an accurate assessment of our spiritual condition. We also have a complex illness that must be prayerfully studied if we seek complete healing. The discouraging and unexpected show of rage (that may or may not have occurred at home, in traffic, or in the office) is not merely an embarrassing failure if we see it as a symptom that helps us to deal with the real problem. Too often we understand sin as doing "bad things," when the truth is that our actions are only the fruit of our sin. The real problem lies in our hearts. We love (read: worship or idolize) peace, food, pleasure, power, fame, security, and approval of people, to name only a few, more than we love God. Until we understand what is at the root of our actions, we will be running in circles, struggling with the same habitual sins.

One way to think of this journey is as a clinical trial where our spiritual symptoms are carefully observed under the care of the Great Physician. If we are willing to look inward and seek the guidance of the Spirit, we will see the major barriers that have obstructed our spiritual growth finally crumble. In my experience, every human being has an inner struggle with a voice that says, "You are not good enough. If people saw the real you, they would walk out on you in disgust." You can imagine how loud this voice

74

must have been in Moses's life. He lived in the palace of Pharaoh, but it is likely people in the palace would have known Moses was really an outsider. His true place was with the Hebrew slaves. One day the tension Moses felt as a result of straddling these two worlds came to a head:

> Years later, when Moses had grown up, he went out to observe his people—*the Hebrews*—and he witnessed the heavy burden of labor forced upon them. He also witnessed an Egyptian beating one of his Hebrew brothers. He looked around *to see if anyone was watching* but there was no one in sight, so he *beat the Egyptian just as the Egyptian had beaten the Hebrew*. *Moses ended up* killing the Egyptian and hid the dead body in the sand.
>
> He went out *again* the next day and saw two of his Hebrew brothers fighting with each other. Moses confronted the offender.
>
> **Moses:** Why are you hitting your friend?
>
> **Offender:** Who made you our prince and judge? Are you going to kill me as you did the Egyptian *yesterday*?
>
> Fear *immediately* gripped Moses.
>
> **Moses** *(to himself)*: The news of what I did must have spread. *I must get out of here quickly.*
>
> *Moses was right.* When the news reached Pharaoh, he sought to have Moses killed. But Moses ran away from Pharaoh until he reached the land of Midian. There he sat down beside a well.[11]

One of the great things about the heroes of the Bible is that when they failed, it was usually epic in nature. In light of Moses killing a man with his bare hands, our momentary rage, irritability, jealousy, and struggle with lustful thoughts seems less horrifying or intimidating. The question is, will we seek to be transformed in ways both large and small and fully become the person we were created to be?

Prayer

God, we thank You for the beauty of Your sacred and divine story. We ask that as we take another step on this sacred journey that we will live more fully in Your hope and grace. Help us to see clearly that we are a people freed from a cruel master. You have paid the price to redeem and free us; may we find that freedom anew as we declare Your lordship in our lives. You are our one true master. Guide us to true freedom.

AUMA IN UGANDA

Auma lives with her father, mother, and three siblings in central Uganda. Her parents work as farmers to grow their own corn, beans, and bananas, and sometimes work helping other farmers. They live in a mud home with a dirt floor and a tin roof. There is no clean water supply close by, so Auma and the other children help out by carrying water. At the church where she receives benefits through Compassion International, Auma likes singing and art. Pray that Auma's parents will encourage her education as she grows up, and will value her ability to learn and become a leader. Pray that her family's crops will grow well, and that they will be a blessing to their neighbors.

Day 7

Do you remember how the children of Jacob (also known as Israel) became slaves in Egypt? At one point they were a wealthy family thriving in their own land with livestock, abundant crops, and enough wealth to buy the favorite son a fancy multi-colored coat. But a famine brought this blessed family a season of scarcity, and when they became fearful that there would not be enough, they turned to Egypt, where their long-lost brother Joseph showed them unexpected favor. That is, until a Pharaoh who did not know Joseph came to power. The children of Israel were no longer grateful workers in the Egyptian empire who received a fair wage for their work; they were a numerous people to be oppressed so that they would be unable to organize and overthrow Pharaoh. The economy became the weapon of their oppression; they literally worked for their dinner. To eat well, they had to work long, hard hours, and any debt would accumulate at an exorbitant rate.

You see the same kind of story in places where modern-day slavery thrives: the sex industry, cacao farms, restaurants, and areas vulnerable to immigration smugglers. You will even find this story emerging in a subtler way in your own neighborhood. Ever thought about what happens to people paying a 37 percent interest rate on their credit card? Ever taken a close look at the fine print details of check-cashing storefronts or the easy way to get a flat-screen television from the local Rent-A-Center? It's not pretty. The change is gradual, but the destination is the same: slavery, working nonstop just to keep your head above the water. Is your work getting the best you have to offer? Do you have anything left? Feel like you are on a treadmill, fighting for survival? Do you ever leave your work behind and take time to rest, relax, worship, and enjoy your friends and family?

I wonder if you remember the last time you laughed yourself sore. The last time that you played with a child and got lost in an imaginary world. The last time you abandoned the need to produce something to be measured by the standards of this world. How often do we hear the equivalent of what the Israelites in Egypt heard: "How many bricks did you make?" "How much money did you make?"

I recently went for a walk with my eight-year-old, and he took me to a wonder-filled place in his imagination. In the middle of our time lost in the woods, I heard this voice, the voice of Pharaoh saying, "What is productive about this?" Where does that voice come from? It is like Pharaoh is implanted in our ears, calling out with demands to produce at all costs.

But as bad as the Israelites' plight was, God allowed it to get worse. As Moses pleaded for their release, God was testing His people:

Pharaoh: Don't supply the people with any more straw to make bricks as you have been doing. Let them go out and find their own straw. But *I still want* you to expect the same number of bricks from them as before. *Even though the task will be harder,* do not lessen their load! They are lazy *and are asking for time off,* saying, "Release us so that we can go sacrifice to our God *in the desert and feast in His honor." Therefore,* make the work so heavy that the men *don't have the energy to do anything but* work; perhaps then they won't be distracted by these lies!

Slave Drivers and Supervisors *(to the people):* Pharaoh has a message for you: "I am not going to supply you with any more straw. You must go out and get it for yourselves—wherever you can find it—*but you must produce the same number of bricks as before.* Your workload will not be reduced."

The people *quickly and desperately* spread out across the land of Egypt looking for dry stalks *of grain* to use for straw. The slave drivers pushed them hard.

Slave Drivers: *Hurry*, you must meet your quotas. You must produce the same number of bricks as you did before when we provided you with straw.

Plus they beat and interrogated the supervisors of the Israelites, the Hebrews whom the slave drivers had appointed over the workers.

Slave Drivers: *Why are you lagging behind?* Why haven't you met your quotas of bricks yesterday or today as you did before?

The supervisors of the Israelites *were unable to meet the demands and so they* appealed to Pharaoh.

Supervisors *(pleading with Pharaoh)*: Why are you treating your servants this way? No more straw is being provided to your servants, yet the slave drivers keep yelling at us, "Make bricks!" And then your servants are beaten; it is your people who are at fault here *not us.*

Pharaoh: *No. It is you.* You are lazy! You are all so very lazy! *You try to escape your work by making up excuses,* saying, "Please release us so that we may go sacrifice to the Eternal." Leave me now, and get back to work, *you indolent whiners!* You will not be provided any straw, and you must make the same number of bricks as before.

The supervisors of the Israelites knew they were in *deep* trouble when they were told, "You are not to lessen the workload. You must still make the same number of bricks every day *as you did before."* After the supervisors left Pharaoh, they went directly to Moses and Aaron who were already waiting for them.

Supervisors *(to Moses and Aaron)*: May the Eternal see and judge what you have done. Now because of you Pharaoh and all who serve him look on us as if we were some kind of disgusting odor. You *might as well* have put the sword in their hands *they will use* to kill us.

Moses went back to *meet with* the Eternal One.

Moses: Eternal, these are Your people. Why have You brought *so much* trouble on them? And why have You sent me here? Ever since I approached Pharaoh to speak in Your name, he has done more harm to them than ever before. And You have done absolutely nothing to rescue Your people.[12]

Despite how it may have seemed to Moses at the time, God had a plan for the lives of His people, one devoted not to an empire but to a new kingdom. He was calling them into a wilderness without food, without water. God said, "I will lead you through this place to a land of promise, and along the way I will supply everything you need. In fact, food will rain from the sky and water will come from rocks. Trust Me, I've got you. I AM everything you need." As you can imagine, removed from their comfort zone, the Israelites struggled to believe and trust God.

Your instinct may be to blame your own idolatries on your job, culture, a crisis, the economy, and everyone else along the way. But when work and material goods become our gods, we are the only ones to blame. This time of fasting is about repentance, and now is as good a time as any.

Prayer

As much as the children of Israel are Your beloved children, we are as well. Forgive us for finding our identity in our vocation or our stuff rather than You. It is so easy to get caught up in making bricks that validate our status to the world, that add to our corporation's profits, or that help us escape the problems in our household. May we put our hand to the plow and work as those who have a higher calling. In the days that come, Lord, reveal to us new patterns of living where our spiritual lives and work lives become an integrated whole. May all that we do be worship to You. Amen.

YEIDY IN COLOMBIA

Yeidy lives with her father, mother, and four brothers and sisters in a coastal Colombian town where fishing is the major industry and where her father has a job. Yeidy helps her mother by cleaning and doing errands at home. An average meal for her family includes fish, corn, and plantains, but clean water and sanitation are big issues in an area where most homes have dirt floors and tin roofs. Yeidy likes playing with dolls and going to school. Pray that Yeidy and her siblings will learn how deeply Jesus loves them, and that living conditions in the community will improve.

Day 8

I have the privilege of being married to the love of my life, Lisa. And I resonate deeply with the way Dr. Iannis describes romantic love to his daughter in the novel *Corelli's Mandolin* by Louis de Bernieres.

> Love is a temporary madness. It erupts like an earthquake and then subsides. And when it subsides you have to make a decision. You have to work out whether your roots have become so entwined together that it is inconceivable that you should ever part. Because this is what love is. Love is not breathlessness, it is not excitement, it is not the promulgation of promises of eternal passion. That is just being "in love," which any of us can convince ourselves we are. Love itself is what is left over when being in love has burned away, and this is both an art and a fortunate accident. Your mother and I had it, we had roots that grew towards each other underground, and when all the pretty blossoms had fallen from our branches we found that we were one tree and not two.[13]

Marriage is the training ground in which many of us learn the challenges of discerning our true affection. It is a universal truth, but I see it most clearly in my marriage, that if my love for God is not exceedingly greater than my love for my wife, my marriage will find itself in troubled waters.

The deficiencies of the English language create problems for us when it comes to the word "love." It is an odd thing, to say the least, that I use the same word to describe my affection for my wife as I do for my affection for nachos. If asked for a list of things I love, within seconds I would tell you God, family, the Houston Astros, Mexican food, and my church. But not always in that order.

It sounds like a joke, but there is more truth here than I care to admit. Imagine my horror when I realized that I am often kinder to my children when the Astros win than in the more likely scenario these days when they lose. Do you realize what that means? I love the Astros too much. The same could be said of Mexican food. I get a bit pouty when I'm not enjoying great food, which is why this journey of fasting is very hard for me. My love of food is also one of the reasons I need to participate in this fast. It is time for me to discover whom or what it is that I truly love. Job had to wrestle with this question: do I love God, or do I only love a God who brings me blessings?

Job had struggles with inner and outer demons on his journey, but I am amazed by his display of faith amid great loss:

And while the words were still leaving that messenger's mouth, *yet* a *fourth* messenger arrived.

Fourth Messenger: All of your children *were gathered together today* under the roof of your firstborn *to celebrate*—eating a feast and drinking wine—and then a powerful wind rose up from *the other side of* the desert, and it struck all four corners of the house. It collapsed! Everyone is dead—all of those young people—*every last one, except me*. I am the only one who got away *from your son's house* to tell you.

Then Job stood up, tore his robe, shaved his head of his hair, and fell to the ground. *Face down*, Job *sprawled in the dirt to* worship.

Job: I was naked, *with nothing*, when I came from my mother's womb;
and naked, *with nothing*, I will return *to the earth*.
The Eternal has given, and He has taken away.
May the name of the Eternal One be blessed.[14]

Our true affections will be exposed on this journey. How are you seeing that happen thus far? Who or what is competing for your affection? Do you see the chaos created when you love anything (even good things: spouse, friends, peace, security, children) more than you love God?

Prayer

God, we pray that You will use this journey to help us see the many things and people that compete for our affections. We are forever grateful that in the midst of sin, You died for us, that though we are broken and we continually fail You and one another, You love us. May that truth go far beyond our heads and into our hearts. May we accept and celebrate that love and in doing so be able to forgive others as You have forgiven us. May we see brothers and sisters in history who have followed You, like Job and know that You have called us to an equally sacred task. You call us out of slavery and oppression and devotion to an empire, and You call us into a new kingdom, a kingdom of abundance and beauty where everyone has enough, where forgiveness and love reign. May we enter those gates this day.

MATHEW IN INDIA

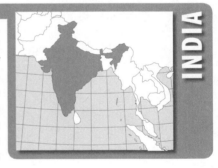

Mathew is twelve years old, so he remembers life before the well. "When I was little, we had to walk from there," he says, pointing down the road toward the neighboring community about a kilometer away. When the Living Water team arrived to drill the well, Mathew remembers jostling with other kids to get a look as the drillers set up the rig and began working.

"Before this," Mathew says, putting his hand on the pump, "we had to wait a long time for water." With several communities sharing a well, lines had been long, and each family could get only a very limited amount of water. This ongoing struggle had hurt the children's education, and their mothers' ability to have family time or earn money. Now, women with wide smiles share that their families are healthier and happier as a result. One family has been able to start a small weaving business. Children like Mathew can go to school instead of walking to the next town to collect water. Pray for the empowerment of people in communities like Mathew's village in India. Pray that clean water will be a stepping-stone toward sustainable development.

Day 9

Ever find yourself speaking up with a boldness you never knew you possessed? Lack of boldness is not my problem, but there are times when I have wondered if I might have been set up by that *Dateline* show where they see who will stand up for a complete stranger.

I am sinner like everyone else, and there are times I unconsciously (as if the car were controlling me) yield to temptation and begin to drive to a place in our city that is a den of gluttony for me. This place, Pancho's, is a Mexican food buffet where I have been known to get more than my money's worth. On one particular day I noticed a man smoking a cigarette in the parking lot while holding a newborn baby in a baby carrier. When I saw him exhale smoke toward the baby, a switch flipped inside me. I made a beeline to him to let him know this was not what a grown man should be doing, and I suggested that he put out his cigarette right away or find somewhere else to smoke. My unwelcome warning did not please him, but after bowing his chest, flexing his arms, and leaning in very close to me, he put out his cigarette.

Lest you misunderstand me, you should know that I am the last guy looking for a fight. Yet, I often experience moments of total clarity when I see someone being abused, oppressed, or mistreated; if the person is weak, I feel a compulsion to stand up for them. Moses was likely to be fearful and intimidated by the grandeur and power of Pharaoh. But God knew that he must speak with an authority that was not his own, and so He gave him a mandate that sounds confusing on the surface but makes perfect sense when we take time to contemplate it.

Eternal One *(to Moses)*: Look! I have made it so that Pharaoh will deal with you as a god and your brother Aaron as your prophet. I want you to tell *Aaron* everything that I command you. Then your brother Aaron will tell Pharaoh to release My people Israel from his land. But I am going to harden Pharaoh's *stubborn* heart so that I can perform sign after sign, wonder after wonder in the land of Egypt. Still Pharaoh will ignore *the message* you *give him*. Then I will unleash the power of My hand against Egypt and liberate My *vast* armies—My people, the children of Israel—from Egypt with *amazing* acts of judgment. When I stretch out My hand against Egypt and free the children of Israel from *their oppressive grasp*, the Egyptians will have no doubt that I am the Eternal.

Moses and Aaron did exactly what the Eternal commanded.[15]

Sounds strange, doesn't it? Pharaoh will deal with you as a god? The Scriptures don't say this kind of thing very often. God is saying, "When you speak, you speak for Me." This is one of the things the church has really missed out on. Some commands in Scripture are so clear that when we talk about them, we ought to speak with a kind of confidence that pushes back the powers of evil and brings comfort to the oppressed. When it comes to those times, when it comes to justice, we speak on behalf of God, and we should do it forcefully. This is about the church stepping forward to keep children from going to bed hungry every night and seeing that those with power do not use it to oppress those without. This about giving all people a place at the table.

What does it look like for each of us to leave the empire and walk toward the kingdom of Christ? It means that we will have to live with the courage of our conviction to speak for God on behalf of those who are suffering.

Prayer

We thank You, God. We thank You that You came to live among us to teach us, to redeem us, to bring salvation where there was oppression. We acknowledge that out of the ashes of our lives You are bringing shalom. We believe You are calling us to be a part of Your shalom work in our own cities and across the globe. We ask You to lead us and guide us. We are called to be Your hands and feet. As representatives of Christ we believe we should carry Your message of love and grace into the dark places You came to restore, the places where disease and illness plague people. Lord, do not allow us to seek safe havens, to hide the news of Your gospel; instead, call us out so that Your Good News will be evident to all. Amen.

RACHEL AND CARLOS IN PERU

Rachel's husband, Mark, poured everything he had into Peru—his love, his passion, his very life. He routinely risked his life to serve the people in the Amazon. He was threatened with death a number of times, but he and Rachel believed Jesus would bring healing and peace wherever needed—and they watched it happen. But when Mark's life was tragically cut short in a motorcycle accident, the light he shone into the dark places of the Amazon seemed in danger of going out. After all, nobody would blame a widow for going home after such a tragedy, but Rachel stayed—and she continues to shine that light. She is committed to the vision she and Mark shared, and she believes in the man who shared their work and their passion, Carlos. Rachel is not giving up, and neither is Carlos. They feel in their souls that they are called to continue proclaiming the gospel among the people they serve. Pray that the light will shine in the darkness as Rachel and Carlos continue to provide clean water in the Amazon.

Day 10

My kids can be picky eaters; more than once I have seen them declare their disdain for a food they have never tried, or refuse to even sample foods of certain colors (read: green). Sometimes it seems as though setting the table is tantamount to setting the stage for an epic battle. They will refuse to eat what is in front of them and still demand that they are hungry, even starving.

I know my kids are not unique in this; I have memories of a grand standoff between my parents and my younger brother. He had a thing with carrots; he would not eat them. I remember feeling a mixture of dread and anticipation when Mom set a bowl of carrots on the dinner table; it was like laying down the gauntlet, a declaration of war. One thing was clear to all of us from the opening bell, I mean prayer: someone was going to win and someone was going to lose.

When you are a parent, one lesson is universal: you must *never* lose this kind of battle. If you do, you have officially lost the upper hand when it comes to everything: bedtimes, homework, manners, you-name-it. My parents understood this rule, and failure was not an option. My brother pouted, cried, threatened (and one time even forced himself to vomit), but he would be at the table for hours until at least a few carrots had been consumed (or possibly hidden). Ironically, that same brother now works at Compassion International, dedicating himself to seeing extreme poverty eradicated in our lifetime and making sure that children have food, education, and health care. Today he sent me a story about a Brazilian boy named Mateus.

Mateus lives in a place called Codó, a forgotten city in the northeast of Brazil, where he and other children wake up each morning without any breakfast. To stave off hunger, they usually drink weak coffee mixed with toasted cassava flour. This mixture, which has no nutritional value, serves only to fill their stomachs for a few hours. Often this breakfast is the only meal they have during the day. Most people live on rice and "cuxa," a food rich in iron but insufficient for a child's nutritional needs.

More than six years ago Compassion sought out Acilâine and her husband, Edivaldo, the pastors of the Evangelical Christian Church in Codó, as partners to love and feed the children of Codó. Thankfully, Mateus, who is only six years old, has attended the project since its inception. At noon each day, Mateus walks past small homes filled with the sounds of scarcity, of small pots boiling an onion sauce or a little bit of rice on a stove made of mud. The strong sunlight forces people to stay home, but this six-year-old makes his way to the place where he hears the sound he most anticipates—the noise of silverware hitting the plates and the clamor of children transforming to complete silence. The children do not speak when they eat. The director says, "They just can't talk when they are lunching. Many of these children were used to eating only cassava flour or bread, or had never used a spoon before. Many of them had never eaten meat, beans, fruits, or salad before." Compassion raises nutritional aid that buys the most basic foods: meat, beans, coffee, and salad. This meal is the only nutrition Mateus receives each day.

I began to read Mateus's story today without knowing it would knock the wind out of me. In the moments before I encountered this child, I had been preoccupied with irritable thoughts and grumblings from my stomach. My pantry is full, and I have more than enough to eat, but like a spoiled child I was not interested in another serving of rice or beans. God help me. I am a selfish man in need of a Savior. A particular parable taught by Jesus came to mind as the kind of reprimand I need.

Jesus: If you want to understand the kingdom of heaven, think about a
king who wanted to settle accounts with his servants. Just as the king
began to get his accounts in order, his assistants called his attention

to a slave who owed a huge sum to him—what a laborer might make in 500 lifetimes. The slave, *maybe an embezzler,* had no way to make restitution, so the king ordered that he, his wife, their children, and everything the family owned be sold *on the auction block*; the proceeds from the slave sale would go toward paying back the king. Upon hearing this judgment, the slave fell down, prostrated himself before the king, and begged for mercy: "Have mercy on me, and I will somehow pay you everything." The king was moved by the pathos of the situation, so indeed he took pity on the servant, told him to stand up, and then forgave the debt.

But the slave went and found a friend, another slave, who owed him about a hundred days' wages. "Pay me back that money," shouted the slave, throttling his friend and shaking him with threats and violence. The slave's friend fell down prostrate and begged for mercy: "Have mercy on me, and I will somehow pay you everything." But the first slave *cackled and was hard-hearted and* refused *to hear his friend's plea.* He *found a magistrate and* had his friend thrown into prison "where," he said, "you will sit until you can pay me back." The other servants saw what was going on. They were upset, so they went to the king and told him everything that had happened.

The king summoned the slave, *the one who had owed so much money, the one whose debt the king had forgiven. The king was livid.* "You slovenly scum," he said, seething with anger. "You begged me to forgive your debt, and I did. *What would be the faithful response to such latitude and generosity?* Surely you should have shown the same charity to a friend who was in your debt."[16]

As one who has received more than I deserve and experienced a grace I could never earn, I feel a bit like this ungrateful servant. May God forgive us for the many times when we turn away from our abundance of rice, beans, bananas, tortillas, or any of the staples that richly sustain us.

Prayer

God, I pray that You will give me eyes to see my abundant blessings. Forgive me for my selfishness and slavery to my own cravings and lead me to see the ways that I can join in Your restorative work in this world. Please be with Mateus and the many children of Codó. God, though they are out of my reach, nothing is beyond Yours. Not their hunger, not my heart. Please take the extra money we have chosen not to spend during this fast and use it for those who are truly hungry. Amen.

JASMINE IN THE PHILIPPINES

Jasmine lives with her parents near the capital city of the Philippines. She carries water and helps her mother in the market. Jasmine's father works part-time to provide the family with the beans, rice, and fish that make up daily meals. The community has a clean water supply, but garbage often collects in the streets and causes pollution. Jasmine is involved at her church, where as a teenager, she has access to vocational training in dressmaking and cosmetology. Pray that she will learn skills that will help her find a good job, and that she will find joy in knowing Jesus.

FEAST DAY: Celebrating Abundance

I had so many amazing friends join me on this fast. They all shared insight, encouragement, and needed wisdom for the journey. I was especially moved by a word from my high school friend turned Episcopal priest Cristopher Robinson. I hope you will take his words to heart as well.

———

Today, like every Sunday, is a celebration of the resurrection, and so we pause in the rhythm of our Lenten fast to enjoy a day to feast instead.

I hope that being on this Lenten journey together has awakened us to our relationship with food in new ways. Approaching the Sundays in Lent this year has reminded me of something I tend to forget about when I'm not fasting: in the world where most of us doing this Lenten fast live—the United States in the twenty-first century—we are blessed with so much abundance in our lives that we have almost forgotten how to *feast*, much less fast.

When we think of the word *feast*, we tend to think about consuming vast amounts of food. We think of Thanksgiving dinner tables groaning under the weight of platters and trays, of scenes in our favorite movies and books, of huge parties and armies of waiters carrying trays piled four feet high with pastries.

But feasting is not about consuming vast quantities. In our world, we can do that practically anytime we want to. I live in a small town in South Texas, and even here there are at least four different all-you-can-eat buffet restaurants. (And they're always crowded!) Most of us routinely keep enough food stored in our pantries and our refrigerators and freezers to feed a small African village.

On our Lenten journey, we have as *much* food as we want. (That's assuming that we all are doing some version of limiting ourselves to eating what is available in the developing world, i.e., eating the foods that the poor eat.) We have plenty of calories and all the nutrients necessary for survival. Ours is a spiritual fast, and there's no reason to be hungry just for the sake of hunger. Of course, we may be getting sick of rice and beans by now, but we have enough to fill our stomachs. Feasting isn't about gorging. It isn't even about "enough."

I have a friend named Clive Berkman who used to own a trendy restaurant in downtown Houston. He published a cookbook titled *Empty Bottle Moments* that tells his life story and gives some of his marvelous recipes. What he strives to create are moments shared by people who love each other, where the conversation is meaningful and the food is delicious and the time spent around the table enriches lives. As he cooked for his friends and family for years, he kept the empty bottles that were all that was left on the table after everything was cleared away—things that symbolize, for him, memorable moments in the richest relationships in life. Bottles empty of wine but overflowing with memory and meaning. Even ordinary meals, he says, can be extraordinary memories.

This is the quality we're looking for in our feasting. Not vast quantities of food but quality of time spent with each other and with God.

This feast day, I invite you to join with me in a prayerful activity that my family observes regularly that I call "eating as a spiritual practice." For one meal, be mindful of offering your labor and the food that you eat to God. Be mindful of the purpose of our fasting: that the food we eat may draw us nearer and nearer into God's presence.

As you prepare to cook, clean the kitchen surfaces that you will use and the table on which you will eat. If you habitually keep them spotless, at least wipe them down with water—this is a spiritual exercise, just as our fast is a spiritual exercise. Ask God to cleanse you and be thankful for the forgiveness we have in Christ Jesus.

When the space is prepared, light a candle, if you have one, somewhere in the kitchen. (I set mine next to the stove.) Let the light be a reminder of God's presence at all times and in all places, but especially in these moments of providing nourishment. When you're done cooking, move the candle to the table.

Whatever you cook, whether it be a new recipe or an old family favorite, whether it be simple (my boys love macaroni and cheese) or complicated, take time for the preparation to be done with care. As you cook, pray for those who will eat it. (If you're single and live alone, pray for yourself!)

Set the table with care. If you have "good" dishes and can reach them easily, get them out. Fold the napkins. Arrange the food carefully on the dishes (yes, even the PB&J sandwiches). Slice. Garnish. Drizzle. Make it as beautiful as you can without going overboard.

Now sit together and pray over the food:

Pray for the farmers who grew it.

Pray for the workers who picked it.

Pray for the truck drivers and sailors who transported it.

Pray for those who inspected it, and for laws and customs that keep us safe and healthy.

Pray for those who own the business from which you bought it, and for their employees.

Pray for the one(s) who cooked it, and give thanks for the people who taught him or her to cook.

And, as always, thank God for the blessing of the food.

Now, sit quietly for a moment, and look at your plate.

Notice the smells (hopefully delicious).

Notice the colors.

Notice how hungry you are, and how your body feels.

All together, take one bite of something. Just one. Savor it. Chew slowly. Be mindful of the texture, the heat or cold, the explosion of taste, especially if you're really hungry. (You may have to explain this part ahead of time.) After the first bite together, everyone may eat closer to their own natural pace. (Slow down if you can, but if you have kids, this will probably be impossible.)

Talk about the ways God has blessed you in the past week. Talk about the things that were delightful. Talk about the things your children did that you were proud of. Tell your loved ones that you love them. And remember that God loves you more than you can imagine.

Prayer

Almighty God, the source of all life and all goodness, we thank You for the blessing of food to sustain us from the bounty of Your creation, and we ask You to make us mindful that our common life together is dependent on the labor of others. We pray in the mighty name of Jesus. Amen.

ABASI IN TANZANIA

Abasi lives with his mother and three siblings in central Tanzania. Their home is a simple mud house with a tin roof and dirt floors. In their dry climate, water is very hard to come by and corn is the main source of nutrition. His mother sometimes finds work helping other people with their farms, but most of her efforts are spent trying to grow food to meet her own family's needs. Abasi helps out by carrying water and firewood. As part of Compassion's ministry, Abasi participates in church activities and Bible classes. Pray that he will be protected from malaria, and that God will bring the resources needed to help the community make better use of their farmland.

Day 11

Moses had a unique perspective on slavery. Like so many of us, he had plausible deniability. It was easy for him to believe that he wasn't a slave when living in Pharaoh's palace. It is easy to believe you are free when your idols are functioning quite well. A month ago I could have said to you (believing that my statement was entirely true) that BBQ Kettle Chips were not a major part of my life. If anyone dared to imply that I love them, much less worship them, I'd have said that you had lost your mind. The truth is that I may be known to turn an almost empty bag inside out to lick the final crumbs out of the bottom. But that is only an indication that I am thrifty, right? That is good steward-ship of potato chips, and we all know those bags have way too much air in them. My Lenten fast has forced me to face the hard facts. I think about eating those chips too often, and my body has a physical response to the thought of those chips. Call it a craving, obsession, or even an addiction; the Bible calls it idolatry. I thought I didn't have a problem because I could eat them whenever I wanted. Now I know.

We, like Moses, have moments of clarity. The individual slave driver is not actually the problem; he will merely be replaced with another. The same can often be true if we simply pursue a modification in our behavior. If we are not careful, we trade one master for another, exchanging this sodium-laced tyrant for an addiction to caffeinated beverages. In the end one is no better than the other.

This fast is beginning to expose our idols. You are likely learning things about yourself that you did not anticipate. That is good; but the journey forward is the key. How will we respond to this newfound clarity?

The Bible talks clearly about masters. Many of us have decided we don't want to be a slave to anything. We don't want to have a master, and we think we can be our own masters. As we discover the idols both large and small that fight for our affection, it is time to affirm that our true master is God. If we miss this transition from our old tyrant to our real master, we will float around with a bunch of other tyrants. Part of what we must understand is that following Christ means He is Lord of our lives. We have a master. We are slaves, but we are slaves to a King who came to liberate humankind. It is paradoxical. We have a master who says, "You are not only My slave but My child and My friend."

Our commitment to follow King Jesus on our own exodus will be tested when we can't always see what God is up to. The path forward will seem dark, scary, filled with unnecessary suffering, even downright insane. Imagine what your moments of doubt may be. What will it take to make you want to turn back? Have you turned back already?

Imagine the struggle when Pharaoh's magicians turned their staffs to serpents. But remember that God's snake eats the others. Don't turn back too quickly.

Forgive me for using casual language to compensate for your natural weakness of human understanding. *I want to be perfectly clear.* In the same way you gave your bodily members away as slaves to corrupt and lawless living and found yourselves deeper in your unruly lives, now devote your members as slaves to right *and reconciled* lives so you will find yourselves deeper in holy living. In the days when you lived as slaves to sin, you had no obligation to do the right thing. *In that regard, you were free.* But what do you have to show from your former lives besides shame? The outcome of that life is death, *guaranteed.* But now that you have been emancipated from the death grip of sin and are God's slave, you have *a different sort of life,* a growing holiness. The outcome of that life is eternal life. The payoff for a life of sin is death, but God is offering us a free gift—eternal life through our Lord Jesus, the Anointed One, *the Liberating King.*[17]

This journey to freedom must begin with a declaration of loyalty to our true master. As we embark, as we cross our own Red Seas, as we see God perform miracles in our own lives to free us from our Pharaohs, may we prepare ourselves for the moments of struggle and doubt that will inevitably come. It is in these moments we will discover our true faith.

Prayer

God, we thank You for the freedom that is found in Christ. All other masters seek to oppress us and steal our joy. You, though, have come to restore us to be the people that You created us to be. Walking away from our comforts is hard. Give to us from Your strength the faith to follow You onto the path that leads us to You. Help us to depend on You, to secure ourselves to You and Your truth that walks alongside us with our questions into the unknown. Cause a craving deep within us for the sustenance in the land of promise. Amen.

SERGIO IN COLOMBIA

Sergio lives in Colombia with his sister and mother, who only works part-time. They live in a rough wood home with a tin roof and dirt floors. Common meals include corn, beans, and bananas. Sergio helps out by gardening, caring for animals in their yard, and making beds. For fun, Sergio likes soccer, singing, and art. Gang violence is a problem in his neighborhood, so Sergio faces pressure from physical poverty and from the attraction of crime as an easy solution. Pray that Sergio will develop lasting relationships at his church that will deepen his faith, and that his family will be protected from violence.

Day 12

If you would have told me as a young boy that I would be able to walk around with a phone in my pocket, I'd have thought you were crazy. Phones have long, curled cords that connect to walls; that's what made Maxwell Smart talking into his shoe so funny (remember that?). But I don't just carry a phone in my pocket. My favorite piece of technology, my iPhone, contains more computing power than the massive servers that were used to launch the first men into space. Of course, most people use it to play Tic-Tac-Toe or Angry Birds, but it is able to speak to satellites in space that can determine where I am standing and the best path to my destination. Mind blowing.

It's easy to read the Exodus narrative and think, "This is a different kind of story set in a different time, and very little of it makes sense today. The world has changed a great deal, and our lives and circumstances seem entirely different from the lives of ancient Hebrews." The truth, though, is that below the surface of our trivial obsessions we are very much like our Israelite ancestors. Their story of liberation holds truths that can lead us to freedom as well.

God had provided everything the Israelites needed, but a famine came, and with it, fear. The children of Israel arrived in Egypt, where the Egyptians had stockpiled food, but they didn't get it for free. They sold themselves for bread and fish. And for almost five hundred years they slaved for Egypt making bricks. Many of us would acknowledge as we review our lives that we have spent much of it making bricks—being a cog in the wheel. We allow our emotional health to rise and fall with the stock market. We wonder what it would be like to make the trip with God's children into a wilderness, where there is nothing, and to learn to trust God to provide everything we need. Are we capable of stepping out into the unknown? That would require faith. Listen carefully: God is calling us to embrace a new way of life in a new economy, a kingdom economy. He will provide everything we need.

It would be nice if the journey of faith were a cakewalk. Truthfully, it is more like an obstacle course or walking the plank! Freedom, though, must be embraced like birth, in stages that bring simultaneous fear and joy. Like the children of Israel who fled from Egypt, you have started the journey by embracing this fast. But as these same children took flight, they also faced near certain death.

Eternal One *(to Moses)*: Speak to the Israelites and tell them to go back and set up camp in front of Pi-hahiroth, between Migdol and the sea, opposite Baal-zephon. Camp there next to the sea. Pharaoh will talk about the Israelites, saying, "They are wandering around in circles. The desert has closed them in *on all sides*." Then I will harden Pharaoh's stubborn heart *even more,* and he will pursue the Israelites. Honor will come to Me through *the actions of* Pharaoh and his army, and the Egyptians will know that I am the Eternal One.

And so they did exactly as the Eternal instructed.

When Egypt's king received the news that the Israelites had run away, the attitude of Pharaoh and his servants changed. They began talking among themselves.

Pharaoh's Servants: What have we done?! We have released the Israelites from serving us *and lost our labor force!*

Pharaoh prepared his chariot and called out his army. He took a select group of the 600 best chariots *in the land* plus all the other chariots in Egypt with drivers commanding all of them.

The Eternal hardened the *stubborn* heart of Pharaoh, king of Egypt; and he chased after the Israelites just as they were marching out of the land with *victorious* hands held high.

The Egyptians pursued the Israelites. All of Pharaoh's horses and chariots, his chariot-drivers and army caught up with the Israelites as they were camping by the sea not far from Pi-hahiroth, opposite Baal-zephon.

Pharaoh approached *the Israelites' camp*, and the Israelites saw the Egyptian army closing in on them. The Israelites *were trapped and* feared for their lives, so they cried out to the Eternal.

Israelites *(to Moses)*: Were there not enough graves in Egypt? Is that why you brought us out here to die in the desert? Why have you done this to us? Why have you made us leave Egypt? Didn't we tell you in Egypt, "Stop pestering us so that we can *get on with our lives and* serve the Egyptians"? It would have been better for us to live as slaves to the Egyptians than to die out here in the desert.

Moses *(to the people)*: Don't be afraid! Stand *your ground* and witness how the Eternal will rescue you today. Take a good look at the Egyptians, for after today you will never see them again.[18]

Here is this mass of people, two million freed slaves, who after sprinting out the door, lose their enthusiasm and begin to roam rather than run. Back in Egypt, Pharaoh is thinking, "The plagues were nasty and I was ready to let them go, but they're just drifting out there without a destination. It would be easy to recapture them." The Hebrews settle in like sitting ducks at the edge of the sea, and God seems to say, "This is where I want you." Absolute vulnerability. Trapped by a mass of water on one side, an army approaching on the other. There is no way out.

Are you feeling trapped by life? Do bankruptcy, broken relationships, sin, destruction, harassment, and failure have you cornered? Congratulations, you are right in the hand of God.

Prayer

God, we thank You that You know right where we are. We thank You that no matter what we have done to distract ourselves from You, You continue to carve out a path should we choose to notice it. In our situations of waiting, may we be aware of Your movements and promptings. Help us continue to step toward freedom.

Reassure us as we look death in the eye, that soon—very soon—
Your hands will open up life in new and unexpected ways. Amen.

SAHID IN SIERRA LEONE

Sahid is a schoolteacher in Sierra Leone. He wears a tie to work and takes his job seriously. Like you, Sahid loves God and his neighbors. Unlike you, his favorite food is monkey. He says it "gives health and vitality." Living Water International may have more water and sanitation expertise than Sahid, but he knows local languages and culture better. He also already has the attention and respect of his students and his village. That's why Living Water partners with teachers like him to carry out sanitation and hygiene programs through schools. In the long run, this approach to training student-leaders in hygiene and sanitation will save even more lives than the clean water they depend on. Pray for Sahid and his students, that their leadership will transform their village in ways only God can imagine. Pray for the implementation of hygiene and sanitation components along with wells that provide clean water.

Day 13

Blaise Pascal once said, "All of man's misfortune comes from one thing, which is not knowing how to sit quietly in a room." No matter how much we have to eat or the infinite choices of reading material at our fingertips, we ultimately drift into a state of boredom. Where does this restlessness come from? Why do I seek diversions so desperately? And when will I, as Augustine says, abandon my restless heart to truly rest in God?

I wish that I could tell you that in my restlessness I turn to prayer each day. The truth is that my daily prayer walk has become essential because it focuses my mind and heart in that direction. Other times? I shuffle through my iPod, surf the internet, read some of yesterday's newspaper, return an endless sea of emails, stare at a wall while listening to CNN, or alternate quickly between varied distractions that present themselves. Have you given up the idol of food only to make your laptop the center of your universe? I'm afraid that I have. If you struggle with this restlessness, you are not alone. In fact, the restlessness we feel can either be the defeat that keeps us in the wilderness or the birthing pangs that bring forth something new within us.

How do we know if our restlessness is instructive (leading us out of the wilderness) or destructive (leading us in circles until we are finally ready to learn)? To answer this question we must search our hearts and study the Scriptures. As we pray for those who are grateful to have any food on their tables, take to heart the words of God, spoken to the prophet Isaiah about a day when all will have the food they need. I pray we are attuned to the ways the kingdom is breaking into our lives as we seek the justice of heaven here on earth.

Eternal One: If you are thirsty, come here;
  come, there's water *for all*.
  Whoever is *poor and* penniless can still
  come and buy *the food I sell*.
  There's no cost—here, have some food, *hearty and delicious,*
  and beverages, *pure and good*.
  I don't understand why you spend your money for things that don't
    nourish
  or work so hard for what leaves you empty.
  Attend to Me and eat what is good;
    enjoy the richest, *most delectable* of things.
  Listen closely, and come *even* closer. My words will give life,
    for I will make a covenant with you that cannot be broken, *a*
    promise
  Of My enduring *presence and* support like I gave to David,
  See, I made him a witness to the peoples, a leader and commander
    among the nations.
  Now you will issue a call to nations *from all over the world*—
    people whom you do not know and who do not know you—
  They will come running, because of *Me*, your God.
    because the Eternal, the Holy One of Israel, has made you
    beautiful.[19]

Our God is near. He sustains with the food we eat and nourishes our souls. May we accept this divine invitation to focus on the Eternal One as He excuses our past wrongs. Thank God for grace.

Prayer

When my life is distracted, when I flip from task to task and nothing piques my interest, remind me, God, to look to You. When I am discontented with what has been given to me and I can't see others because I am so far away within myself—remind me, God, to come before You. Remind me to look toward You and breathe deeply. To let You hold me and speak to me about the distractions. Thank You for all of the gifts You have given me. As You remind me of Your place in my life, may all the distractions fall into theirs. Let me see my shortcomings clearly, God. Show me all the sins You have covered for me so I would not be afraid to seek the path of redemption. Remind me that You are plentiful. That You are more than enough for all, that You meet me in intimate ways even as I divert myself. Amen.

RONALD IN UGANDA

Ronald lives with his uncle in central Uganda, near Lake Victoria. His uncle has part-time work as a laborer, and Ronald helps at home by carrying water, gathering firewood, and gardening. As part of Compassion's ministry, Ronald participates in church activities and choir. He is also in vocational training, where he is doing very well. Soccer and running are some of his favorite activities. It is very humid and hilly where Ronald lives, and the soil is fertile. Potatoes, corn, and beans are included in most meals. However, malaria is a constant threat, and bad drinking water causes many stomach problems. Pray that Ronald will stay healthy and will learn how to teach others about good sanitation and disease prevention.

Day 14

I love the feeling I receive from a job well done. There is nothing like finishing a project or celebrating an outcome that once seemed impossible. Conversely, I dread the taste of failure or a missed opportunity. I perpetually forget that today's fiasco is setting the stage for tomorrow's victory. The two go hand in hand.

A few days ago we left Moses and his crew, two million strong, when they were backed into a corner. It was just where they needed to be, but that truth is hard to believe when it comes to the way we live. One of the reasons we despise weakness in ourselves is that it forces us to rely on one another and God to find the strength to move forward. When I operate out of weakness rather than power, as I have in these last two weeks, I get a taste of what God is capable of doing through me. You don't hear many sermons on the way Jesus began His movement—by inviting followers to embrace a voluntary poverty. It does not fit in our Western models of ministry, but it will help us to find comfort in these minimal sacrifices we are making during this fast.

The Lord then recruited and deployed 70 more disciples. He sent them ahead, in teams of two, to visit all the towns and settlements between them and Jerusalem. This is what He ordered.

Jesus: There's a great harvest waiting in the fields, but there aren't many good workers to harvest it. Pray that the Harvest Master will send out good workers to the fields.

It's time for you 70 to go. I'm sending you out *armed with vulnerability*, like lambs walking into a pack of wolves.[20]

We have a tradition at my church, Ecclesia. Whenever we begin a new small group, the people in that group take the time over a long dinner for each person to share their life story. This kick-starts a sense of community in many ways. But what it does most is invite people to relate to one another out of their weakness rather than strength. Everyone is afraid to tell their story in a way that is totally truthful because we all have this deep-seated fear that if people really knew us, they would reject us. So everyone trembles, and some call me for permission to give the PG version of their life (I don't give it), and after threatening to cancel the meeting entirely, they spill their souls despite worries that their new friends will storm out of the room when they hear who they are and what they have done. The opposite always happens; as people get to these hard places in their story, the chairs begin to inch closer together. People are saying with their body posture, "I'm not going to leave you, and I love you more when I see the real you."

Living out of weakness does not mean we become martyrs who have nothing and do nothing. God has created us for a beautiful life, not one filled with stress and anxiety. As we peel back the layers of failures, projections of confidence, hidden fears, and endless distractions, we are much more likely to find that life.

I want to remind you today, nearly halfway through this fast, to care well for yourself on this journey. As your weaknesses are exposed, you are learning, and one thing we all need to learn is how to care well for ourselves. Take the time you need for that quiet prayer walk, read an enjoyable book, and find time to laugh. You may not be able to eat chocolate during these days, but don't deprive yourself of laughter.

Prayer

God, we thank You for leading us into our weakness so that we can escape the burden of constant stress and anxiety over the many things we cannot control. We are learning, and will continue to learn in the days to come, how to trust You for everything we need.

*We thank You for the abundance of food we have, and we ask
Your forgiveness when we treat it as anything less than a blessing.
May the food we eat and the water we drink in the coming days
taste so much sweeter because we realize so clearly that it comes
from You. Amen.*

THE DAGARA TEAM IN BURKINA FASO

In 2010, Living Water International began a partnership with the Dagara Team, a vibrant church-planting movement in Burkina Faso. In a region where Jesus was previously unknown, some thirty churches have been planted and new ones spring up with astounding regularity. Water ministry has enhanced the emerging church's capacity to heal the sick and love the least of their brothers and sisters. The Bible doesn't yet exist in the Dagara language, but the church is expanding at incredible rates through very personal, tangible acts of love. And when Dagara people see fellow Dagarans take on the biggest life-and-death problems in their communities—like water—they naturally want to know even more about the living water these disciples talk about. Pray that water ministry will continue to open doors for the message of Jesus among the Dagara people and all people who have never heard the Good News.

Day 15

Even if you were not a person of faith, you would likely declare the book of Exodus one of the best, most miraculous, most beautiful stories ever told. For people of faith, it is not just a story—this is God's people being guided and led. We have so much to learn from them. We've stood at the water's edge with God's children completely surrounded by the sea in front of us and Pharaoh's army pressing in behind us. We talked about how being in this place, this place of utter helplessness where God must intervene, is where we thrive. I don't really want to be here, vulnerable and surrounded on all sides, but I have seen too many times on my journey that I have to come to a place where I realize I need to be rescued. I often think that God is waiting until the very last moment, but the truth is that I am the one holding out for a way that my plan might come together. God has only been waiting for my surrender.

Real justice and freedom from oppression come only from the hand of God, usually in a way that is clear man did not orchestrate it. Moses can't get the credit along the way because it is clear to all people that rescue has come by divine, not human, hands. So the journey we are on with God's children is one out of Egypt, out of oppression, out of slavery—a journey from a place where our lives are devoted to all the wrong things into freedom and abundance, in a land where God provides for us.

Moses *(to the people)*: Don't be afraid! Stand *your ground* and witness how the Eternal will rescue you today. Take a good look at the Egyptians, for after today you will never see them again. The Eternal will fight on your behalf while you watch in silence.

Eternal One *(to Moses)*: Why do you call for Me? Instruct the Israelites to *break camp and* keep moving. Raise your staff and reach out over the sea to divide it. The Israelites will be able to walk straight through the sea on dry ground. I am going to harden the *stubborn* hearts of the Egyptians, and *in their arrogance* they will continue to chase the Israelites. My honor will be on display *when I defeat* Pharaoh, his army, his chariots, and his chariot-drivers. The Egyptians will know that I am the Eternal when I display my glory through Pharaoh, his chariots, and his chariot-drivers.

God's messenger, who had been out front leading the people of Israel, moved to *protect* the rear of the company; the cloud pillar moved *with him* from the front to the back of them. The cloud pillar took its position between Egypt's and Israel's camps. The cloud cast darkness *by day* yet it lit up the sky by night. As a result, the Egyptians never got close to the Israelites the entire night. Moses then *took his staff and* reached out over the sea. The Eternal parted the sea with a strong east wind, which blew all night and turned the floor of the sea into dry ground between the divided waters. The Israelites *broke camp and* traveled on dry ground through the parted waters, and the sea stood like a *solid* wall on their right and on their left.

The Egyptians *were undaunted. They* continued their pursuit— all of Pharaoh's horses, chariots, and chariot-drivers—followed the Israelites into the middle of the sea.

Before daybreak the Eternal peered down upon the Egyptian army through the fire pillar and the cloud pillar and threw them all into confusion. He caused the wheels of their chariots to break down so that it was nearly impossible for the drivers to control them. *The Egyptians knew something was wrong.*

Egyptians: Let's go and get away from these Israelites. *Their God,* the Eternal One, is fighting for them against us.

After all the Israelites had reached the other side of the sea, the Eternal spoke to Moses.

Eternal One *(to Moses)*: *Now take your staff and* reach out over the sea. The waters *which I parted* will crash upon the Egyptians and cover their chariots and chariot-drivers.

So Moses raised his hand and reached out over the sea, *and the walls of water collapsed.* As dawn gave way to morning, the sea returned to normal and the Eternal swept the retreating Egyptian army into the sea. The waters rushed and covered all the chariots and their drivers, swallowing up all of Pharaoh's army that had pursued Israel into the sea. Not one Egyptian survived.

But the Israelites had walked *safely* through the parted waters on dry ground, and the sea stood like a *solid* wall on their right and on their left. That day the Eternal rescued Israel from the *powerful* grip of the Egyptians, and Israel watched the corpses of the Egyptians *wash up* on the shore. When Israel witnessed the incredible power that the Eternal used to defeat the Egyptians, the people were struck with fear of Him, and they trusted in Him and also in Moses, His servant.[21]

True rescue is a thing of beauty. Can you imagine the rush of joy God's children experienced as they passed through the waters on dry land? Do you remember watching helicopters lift the residents of New Orleans off the roofs amid the devastation of Hurricane Katrina? I remember watching a young family as they were hoisted to safety. I wondered how I would seek to repay my rescuers for saving my children.

We worship a God of rescue. In the midst of the destruction of sin, often of our own choosing, He has pursued us with an unyielding forgiveness. It is time we surrender and place ourselves in the strong and faithful arms of a God who has been waiting patiently.

Prayer

God, we thank You for saving our lives. That when we are in tight situations, when we cannot find a way out, You trench out a path with hope that we will leave our own ways for Yours. Anything we can manage is but a quick fix; Yours is a permanent resolve. You have made a direct path to You just like when You pulled back the sides of the sea so many years ago. We can't build our way to

111

You, though we are good at making bricks. We can't suffer our way to You, although we are good at punishing ourselves and others. Your way is Jesus. May we lay our ways down on this side of the sea and step onto the dry ground that always leads to You. Amen.

TATIANA IN ECUADOR

Tatiana lives with her mother in a very poor coastal area in southern Ecuador. The city is without good basic sanitation or clean water, and crime is an everyday occurrence. Bronchitis, parasite infections, and dengue fever are common illnesses among Tatiana and the other children in her neighborhood. Her mother doesn't have full-time work and relies on support from Compassion and her local church. As part of Compassion's ministry, Tatiana participates in Bible classes and enjoys singing and art. Pray that in a place of brokenness and extremely difficult living conditions, God will show His love and faithfulness to Tatiana. Pray that she will find beauty in her surroundings and grow to become a young woman who brings joy and healing to her community.

Day 16

How do you respond to undeserved grace? If you have been given a gift of true rescue, how do you express your gratitude? The passage below may not be the climax of the story, but it is the most uplifting passage in the entire narrative. Grateful people offer sincere thanks to God. The words themselves breathe comfort and joy into me. This is the first song, or first psalm, recorded in all the Scriptures. Moments after God provided this miracle of rescue, the natural response of these broken people was to worship. And worship does a lot of things: it focuses us on what is eternal, it draws us close to God, it reminds us of what God has done. This is why we sing songs when we gather—because our faith is increased as our spirits remember. Today many of us need to look beyond the waters and the approaching armies to see the God who is coming to save. Worship focuses us on that.

I want to encourage you to read reflectively this first song by Miriam today. Be guided by the Spirit. Let your ears hear it and let the Spirit allow the words and phrases to come through to you today. God has a message for us in this text to bring us back to the right path.

Moses and the Israelites sang this song to the Eternal One.

Moses and the Israelites: I will sing to the Eternal, for He has won a great victory;
> He has thrown the chariot into the sea: horse and rider.
The Eternal is my strength and my song,
> and He has come to save me;
He is my God, and I will praise Him.
> He is the God of my father, and I will exalt Him.

The Eternal is a warrior;
the Eternal is His name.
Pharaoh's chariots and his army He has thrown into the sea.
And his high-ranking officers are drowned in the Red Sea.
The deep waters covered them;
they sank to the *muddy* depths like a stone.
Your right hand, Eternal One, is magnificent in power.
Your right hand, Eternal, vanquishes the enemy.
In Your majestic greatness You conquer those who rise against You;
You unleash Your burning anger, and it consumes them like
straw.
With a blast of Your anger the waters piled high,
the waves stood up like a wall;
in the heart of the sea, deep waters turned solid.
The enemy said, "I will go after them, chase them down, and divide
the spoils;
my desire will be spent on them.
I will draw my sword; my powerful hand will take possession of
them *once again*.
But You blew Your breath-wind, and the sea covered them;
they sank like lead down into the mighty waters.
Who compares to You among the gods, O Eternal?
Who compares to You—great in holiness,
awesome in praises, performing *marvels and* wonders?
You raised Your right hand,
and the earth swallowed Your enemies.
With Your loyal love, You have led the people You have redeemed
with Your great strength You have guided them to Your sacred
dwelling.
Already people have heard and they tremble;
those who inhabit Philistia are gripped by fear.
Even now the chiefs of Edom are deeply disturbed;
Moab's leaders cannot stop trembling;
all who live in Canaan are *deeply distressed and* wasting away.
Horror and fear overwhelm them.
Faced with the greatness of Your power,
people are afraid to move, *they fall as silent* as stone,
Until Your people pass by, Eternal One,
until the people whom You purchased pass by.

You will bring them and plant them on the mountain of Your
   inheritance—
   the place, Eternal, that You have designated to be Your dwelling,
   the sanctuary, Lord, that Your hands founded *and made ready.*
   The Eternal will reign *as King* forever and always.

When Pharaoh's horses, chariots, and chariot-drivers drove into the
sea, the Eternal caused the waters to collapse upon them. But the
Israelites walked through the sea on dry ground.[22]

Take some time to sing today. It may be on a walk or when
you're alone in your car, but express your thanks to God and let
your heart fill with joy.

Prayer

*God, hear our voices! We thank You that You have called us into
the same creative expression You used to bring all things to life:
song. You have made us to reflect love, so today, may our response
to Your rescue be hearts filled with delight. Help us to see Your
bountiful provision today and celebrate. We are learning to remember those who are suffering as we lean more fully into this fast. We
pray that it changes us. Amen.*

KEILA IN COLOMBIA

COLOMBIA

Keila lives with her mother and four brothers and sisters in northeastern Colombia. She helps out around their simple home by making beds, working in the kitchen, and cleaning. Her mother does not have a full-time job, so the help Keila receives through Compassion and her local church is crucial. Playing with dolls, jumping rope, and playing ball games are Keila's favorite activities. In school she is an average student, but poor nutrition and regular illness make it hard for Keila and other students to learn well. Pray that Keila will have new opportunities to learn and grow physically, mentally, and spiritually, and that her mother will find a steady job.

FEAST DAY: Celebrating the Journey

The story of the Lamb is a long story through Scripture that begins in Genesis and goes to the end of Revelation. This story depicts our longing for deliverance, the atonement for our sin, and the celebration of God's grace. We are a people awaiting and expecting the arrival of the Lamb.

In Genesis 22, we have the story of Abraham and Isaac, a story that is difficult for many of us Western, modern people to understand. Abraham is journeying with Isaac, and God says to him, "I know you have waited for this son, I know that you believe the hopes for your life are dependent on this son, but your children belong to Me. I want you to take him to the altar of sacrifice because you have sinned, Abraham." Part of what we don't understand is the reason why Abraham doesn't fight God on this: it isn't because he doesn't love his son but because he understands that God has to be a just god. Abraham has no doubt about the fact that he has sinned and that a sacrifice has to be made. If you look at the story of Abraham, you see him make mistakes time and time again just like you and I do.

The most challenging part of the story for us is when Isaac walks with Abraham toward the altar. You can just see his little mind turning, putting the pieces together. "I know we are going to make a sacrifice, but where is the lamb?" And Abraham says, "God will provide." Hoping against hope that he won't have to sacrifice his son, Abraham makes it all the way to the altar, and God says,

"Stop." But God provides a ram, not a lamb and so enters the tension of the story—the awaiting of the sacrificial lamb.

And then here in Exodus, God comes to rescue His people and says, "Take the lamb, roast it, eat it, put its blood on your door posts because this is what is going to happen . . . I am going to pass through during the night as judge. I don't normally come as judge, but I will come as the breath of death." God is coming to rescue the Israelites, and His coming is marked with the sacrifice and feast of the lamb.

Eternal One *(to Moses and Aaron in the land of Egypt)*: Mark this month as the first month of all months for you—the first month of your year. Declare this message to the entire community of Israel: "When the tenth day of this month arrives, every family is to select a lamb, one for each household. If there aren't enough people in the family *to eat* an entire lamb, then they should share a lamb with their nearest neighbor according to how many people are in the neighbor's family. Divide the portions of the lamb so that each person has enough to eat. Choose a one-year-old male that is intact and free of blemishes; you can take it from the sheep or the goats. Keep this chosen lamb safe until the fourteenth day of the month, then the entire community of Israel will slaughter their lambs *together* at twilight. They are to take some of its blood and smear it across the top and down the two sides of the doorframe of the houses where they plan to eat. That night, have them roast the lamb over a fire and feast on it along with bitter herbs and bread made without yeast. Do not eat any meat raw or boil it in water; only eat the meat after the *entire* animal has been roasted over a fire with its head, legs, and intestines attached. *Eat whatever you can,* but don't leave any of it until morning; whatever is left over in the morning burn in the fire. Here is how *I want you* to eat this *meal*: Be sure you are dressed and ready to go *at a moment's notice*—with sandals on your feet and a walking stick in your hand. Eat quickly because this is My Passover.

I am going to pass through the land of Egypt during the night and put to death all their firstborn children and animals. I will also execute *My* judgments against all the gods of the Egyptians, for I am the Eternal One! The blood on *the doorframes of* your houses will be a sign of where you are. When I *pass by and* see the blood, I will pass over you. This plague will not afflict you when I strike the land of Egypt *with death.*

This will be a day for you to always remember. I want you and all generations after you to commemorate this day with a festival to Me. Celebrate this feast as a perpetual ordinance, *a permanent part of your life together.*[23]

When God finally delivers His people, He declares that all are to join in a sacred barbecue. Have you ever had roasted lamb? When lamb is cooked slowly over the fire as God instructs, it is a remarkable meal. This sacred feast is an important part of our liturgy as followers of Jesus. It is this meal that Jesus asks each of us to observe as a remembrance of His sacrificial love for us. As Jesus gathers the disciples for a Passover meal, they are seated around a table with bread and wine. You can imagine that the disciples had all sorts of questions in their minds: Where is the lamb? Has Jesus forgotten the main course? How can we celebrate Passover without the lamb? But the message ultimately becomes clear: Jesus is the Lamb and He came to be slain for our deliverance.

When we feast together as followers of Christ we are participating in the sacred feast of the Lamb. We have so much to celebrate as people who have been rescued from bondage. Raise your glass today and give thanks for the remarkable blessing of the Lamb.

Prayer

God, we thank You for becoming the Lamb who wipes away our sins. As we join in the ancient practices of our faith by eating together and giving thanks for Your miraculous rescue of each of us, we enjoy the flavors of the food placed before us. Like the Israelites, we are also dining with our shoes on and our bags packed, because You are also taking us on a journey. May we be ready to receive the wisdom that You have for each of us on this grand adventure. Amen.

TAHIR IN INDIA

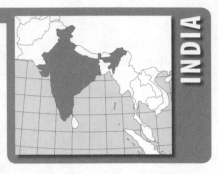

Tahir lives with his parents in India. He helps at home by carrying water and by sewing. His father sometimes finds part-time work as a common laborer and his mother stays at home. The community is dirty and congested, with no good water supply and poor sanitation. Most homes are made of mud, sticks, and leaves. The nearest hospital is a two-hour walk away. Tahir likes to play ping-pong and soccer with friends at the church where he receives support from Compassion. Pray that Tahir will do well in school and overcome the illiteracy that has held his parents back. Pray that he and his friends will transform their community as they grow and become leaders who love Jesus.

Day 17

With songs of celebration and praise still ringing in the air, the attention of God's children began to shift once again from victorious rescue to the new challenges of the wilderness. As we've seen, they move from being grateful for God's miraculous provision to doubt and disbelief as they cry out to God in anger, "Why didn't we just die in Egypt!"

> Then the entire community of Israel departed from Elim and entered the desert of Sin, which is located between Elim and Sinai. *They arrived there* on the fifteenth day of the second month after they had departed from Egypt.
> *As soon as* they got to the desert *of Sin*, the entire community of Israelites complained to Moses and Aaron.

Israelites: It would have been better if we had died by the hand of the Eternal in Egypt. At least *we had plenty to eat and drink, for* our pots were stuffed with meat and we had as much bread as we wanted. But now you have brought the entire community out to the desert to starve us to death.

Eternal One *(to Moses)*: Look! I will cause bread to rain down from heaven for you, and the people will go out and gather a helping of it each day. I will test them to see if they are willing to live by My instructions.[24]

Almost all of us suffer from a sort of spiritual amnesia—God does miraculous and beautiful things that somehow we easily forget. The Israelites' circumstances were so dire that God had to step in and defy the laws of physics, parting the sea and collapsing it on Pharaoh's army. In all the excitement of the miraculous exit there was no time to stock up on snacks for the road trip. But don't you think their faith in God's provision would be soaring at this point?

We aren't so different from the Israelites. God provides all we need, and yet we tremble in fear when a new challenge rears its head. It makes no sense. It would be like Lazarus being raised from the dead and a week later hearing him scream, "God, where are You? You have abandoned me. That raised-from-the-dead thing was last week . . . what are You going to do for me today?!"

My prayer is that the Scriptures will help us remember where we came from. When I do weddings, I like to pray with both the bride and groom before the wedding. My prayer for them is that they would somehow be able to turn on a recorder in their mind that will help them remember with all their senses this remarkable moment—the love they share, the smell of the flowers, the taste of their first kiss as husband and wife. I want this for them because I know that in the next few days, weeks, or months they will have moments when they forget every bit of that. And they will desperately need to return to this place. They will need to stop and remember their love for one another.

It would be wonderful if every day was your wedding day, but marriage does not work that way. Life and faith do not work that way either. We would love to live on a constant spiritual high, but God does not part the sea every day. It is a once-in-a-lifetime event that we have to cling to as a reminder of God's love and grace. There will be ups and downs. The trouble is, if you can't remember the ups, the downs feel really low.

How can we focus our hearts on God's grace and take our faith into the challenges we face with a confidence that God will take care of us? Consider praying the Lord's Prayer today. It is a reminder that we are not called to store up our provision for the year. Interpretations of "Give us this day our daily bread" vary, but one thing is clear: when we have everything we need, it becomes easy to believe we do not have to trust in God. Can you imagine the discipline needed for the children of Israel to take only the manna they needed for that day? They wondered every night whether God would provide for them the next day. He did for them, and He will for us.

Prayer

Our Father, who art in heaven, hallowed be Thy name. Thy kingdom come. Thy will be done, on earth as it is in heaven. Give us this day our daily bread, and forgive us our trespasses, as we forgive those who trespass against us. And lead us not into temptation, but deliver us from evil. For Thine is the kingdom, and the power, and the glory, forever and ever. Amen.

TAMARAH IN HAITI

Tamarah lives with her mother and father on the eastern edge of Port-au-Prince, Haiti. She helps out at home by carrying water and washing clothes. Her father looks for part-time work as a common laborer and her mother sometimes sells fruit and vegetables in the local market. Tamarah is like many young children and enjoys playing jacks, singing, and playing house. She attends church activities, Bible class, and Vacation Bible School. On an average day she might eat beans, rice, and bananas, but malnutrition is a constant threat because of high food prices and lack of jobs. Pray that as Tamarah grows she will avoid illness from intestinal worms, and that her parents will find enough work to provide food.

Day 18

Have you ever been ensnared by a natural disaster or poor planning on a hike and experienced the panic of trying to find water? In the physical realm there is nothing more valuable, and nothing we seem to take for granted more, than water. I'll never forget a conversation I had in a remote village on the west coast of Africa with a woman who was thunderstruck by rumors that we in the West use clean water to flush our toilets and water our lawns. Water is so precious to her that she would walk miles to draw it from an unsanitary river. When clean water came to her village as a result of a movement to recapture the beauty of Christmas (www.AdventConspiracy.org), it brought with it the power to eliminate the cholera, disease, sickness, and diarrhea that was needlessly stealing the life of children.

The water crisis is at the heart of a daily emergency faced by a billion of the world's most vulnerable people—a crisis that threatens life and destroys livelihoods on a devastating scale. Unlike war and terrorism, the global water crisis does not make media headlines, despite the fact that it claims more lives through disease than any war claims through guns. Unlike natural disasters, it does not rally concerted international action, despite the fact that more people die each year from drinking dirty water than from the world's hurricanes, floods, tsunamis, and earthquakes combined. This is a crisis that is holding back human progress, consigning large segments of humanity to lives of poverty, vulnerability, and insecurity. The church can see an end to this silent crisis experienced by the poor and tolerated by those with the resources, technology, and the political power to end it.

As Moses leads God's children to a land of promise, they make camp in an area with no access to fresh water. Despite their history of experiencing God's radical provision, they begin to panic. It starts with grumbling, doubt, and disbelief:

> The entire community of Israel traveled in stages out of the desert of Sin, just as the Eternal instructed. They camped at Rephidim, but there was no water there to quench their thirst. *Once again* the people complained to Moses.

Israelites: Give us water to drink! *We're thirsty.*

Moses: Why do you aim your complaints at me? Why are you testing the Eternal One?

> But the people were so thirsty for water, they complained to Moses *and leveled accusations against him.*

Israelites: Why did you lead us out of Egypt? Was it to kill *all of* us—our children and livestock included—with this thirst?

> Moses *had had enough of their complaints, so he* cried out to the Eternal One.

Moses: What am I supposed to do with these people *and their relentless complaining?* They are on the verge of stoning me.

Eternal One (to Moses): *Here's what I want you to do:* go on ahead of the people and take some of the elders of Israel with you. *Also,* be sure to bring your *shepherd's* staff—the one with which you struck the Nile. I will be there when you arrive standing at the rock of Horeb. I want you to strike the rock *with your staff*; and *when you do,* water will flow out of it so that everyone will have *enough* to drink.

> The elders of Israel *accompanied Moses and* watched as he did what the Eternal directed.[25]

It is awe inspiring to see God use the staff of Moses as the instrument of rescue. God has given us a command to care for the thirsty too. When we are obedient, as Moses was, it is a beautiful thing.

Recently our church stumbled into a relationship with a tribal king in Nigeria. He spoke to us of the tremendous need in his kingdom for clean water. In a very specific area, more than twenty thousand people were suffering. Two previous governmental attempts to drill wells had been unsuccessful. Any attempt to drill deep enough to strike water would be both costly and risky. Is there anything more depressing than a dry hole that cost $70,000 to drill and a kingdom of thirsty people?

At my church, we prayed about the situation and consulted with our partners at Living Water International, and then we took a step of faith and decided to try to bring clean water to these Nigerian brothers and sisters in the name of Jesus. The staff we used in this case was an Ingersoll Rand TH60 Truck Mounted Rig—a bit more sophisticated than Moses's staff but much less mysterious. The Living Water team drilled 250 meters through layer after layer of rock, destroying a roller cone and rock bit in the process. We struck again and again, wrestling with the earth, believing that God would bring forth clean water. We called friends across the globe when it looked like we were facing another fruitless attempt to deliver these brothers and sisters from the hardships of not having sanitary water. But in the end, we were able to give them clean water in the name of Jesus—enough to provide for nine villages and ten clans.

Prayer

God, we thank You for the gift of clean water. Forgive us when we grumble and complain despite the abundant blessings that surround us. Help us to remember the amazing event of Moses at the Rock of Horeb so that our hearts are grateful when we encounter clear, clean water in our lives. Inspire us to continue to work alongside You to share this gift with those who have not. May we be a people celebrating Your miracle of provision for 2 million in the wilderness,

20,000 in Nigeria, and the places that You will lead us in the days to come to share Your love and grace. Amen.

PABLO IN ECUADOR

Pablo is a teenager who lives with his parents and two siblings in the mountains of central Ecuador. His father works as a farmer, but the local wheat, barley, and quinoa crops do not produce enough to adequately support the families in the area. On a typical day Pablo might eat corn, potatoes, and bread, but malnutrition and respiratory infections are serious health issues. Pablo helps out at home by carrying water and firewood, and washing clothes. He likes to play soccer with his friends and enjoys singing at church. Please pray that God will keep Pablo healthy. Pray that he will be a good example to younger children around him, and that he will become a leader who helps provide new educational and job opportunities in the community.

Day 19

So far in the Exodus and Numbers narrative, we have encountered extreme examples of how hard our hearts can become, lacking even an ounce of gratitude or memory. These passages can be dangerous to the reader. If we are not careful, we start to feel pretty good about ourselves in comparison to the Israelites. If we read this story in that way, our prayer at the end will end up sounding like that of the Pharisee who "stands up and prays this prayer in honor of himself: 'God, how I thank You that I am not on the same level as other people—crooks, cheaters, the sexually immoral—like this tax collector over here.'"[26]

It is easy to judge God's children as they complain about their situation. How could anyone be so selfish? God is raining down nutritious food from the sky to sustain them in the wilderness, and they are complaining about the menu? They don't pay for it, plant it, or harvest it. God is guiding them with unimaginable miracles to a land of promise, and they make slavery in Egypt sound like Disneyland. They dream of turning back to their slave masters so they can enjoy fish, garlic, and onions again.

These people were insane—and so are we. We need storage buildings to hold our extra things that do not fit in the garage, and yet we fix our attention on the next item we *must* possess—a laptop, phone, car, house, clothes, shoes. The items vary, but you can bank on it: something will capture our affection and the world will not seem right until we have it. How often have we been tempted to complain during this fast or give up because it is just too hard? I have been guilty of both.

The passage below is very convicting when we read it as a mirror into our own souls. Talking about those sinful people ("Can you believe what they did?!") is not so fun when we realize we are farther off the path than they were.

Let's face it. People could close a book of our life stories and say the same thing: "What were they thinking?" Paul was no stranger to this feeling.

Listen, I can't explain my actions. Here's why: I am not able to do the things I want; and at the same time, I do the things I despise. If I am doing the things I have already decided not to do, I am agreeing with the law regarding what is good. But now I am no longer the one acting—*I've lost control*—sin has taken up residence in me *and is wreaking havoc.* I know that in me, that is, in my fallen human nature, there is nothing good. I can will myself to do something good, but that does not help me carry it out. I can determine that I am going to do good, but I don't do it; instead, I end up living out the evil that I decided not to do. If I end up doing the exact thing I pledged not to do, I am no longer doing it because sin has taken up residence in me.[27]

Prayer

God, I am thankful that Your ancient words continue to enlighten my life. Please strengthen my posture, that when I pick up Your book, I not only enjoy the amazing story and people of the past, but I draw the lessons into my own life. Let these words unfold within my heart as a letter of encouragement from You to me. It is not by my strength but Yours that I am able to be truly vulnerable to love and able to give compassion to myself and others when we miss the mark. May my life be shaped by thankfulness and a vision for life as a kingdom citizen where all are equal and welcome. Amen.

FELIPE IN GUATEMALA

Felipe lives with his parents and one sibling in western Guatemala. Both of his parents find part-time work but like many people in the community struggle to make ends meet. Corn, beans, and bananas are part of Felipe's daily diet. He helps at home by caring for animals and cleaning, but he is still young and prefers to play with cars. Pray that conditions in the community will improve and his parents will find consistent work. Pray that Felipe will become a good student who loves God, and will think creatively about how to provide jobs in his community and country.

Day 20

One type of sin is particularly contagious. It is an infection with great resilience that spreads quickly among people, despite the availability of an effective vaccine (more on that tomorrow). I'm speaking of grumbling, whining, and gossiping. Part of the reason the children of Israel were stuck in the wilderness on a 40-year journey that could have ended in a week is because they were obstinate, grumbling people. Nothing ever seemed to be good enough to fully satisfy them; they complained about everything, even though God provided for them daily. Basically all they had to do for dinner was pick up the bread God blanketed the earth with the night before.

In my opinion, the sin of grumbling or ingratitude and her ugly twin sister gossip are radically contagious sins. When someone comes to you and starts complaining, it is easy to get sucked in. It seems like the moment you start grumbling or whining, a chemical release happens in your brain that gives you a momentary high.

We understand we are all sinners in need of God's grace. Yet in the New Testament Paul is really clear: if you find someone who is complaining and grumbling, gossipy and divisive, go and rebuke that brother or sister once, and if they don't listen to you, be done with them. What! Really? You could be a struggling alcoholic and a community will walk with you, but a grumbling, complaining person is to be ejected? To be clear, we are not talking about constructive criticism or thoughtful complaints—we are talking about gossip and murmuring. If you call over the manager at a restaurant because there is a hair in your salad, you are helping them to know that someone needs to wear a hairnet. A word of critique is

131

necessary at times as we all work toward improving our lives. Our problem is that we fall too easily into selfish criticism.

What are the things you grumble about? Money? Schedules? Someone else's mess? Time changes? Work and traffic? Co-workers? Family? Grumbling is a real problem that grows out of dissatisfaction. It brings down the complainer, and it also spreads like a plague.

The people griped *about life in the wilderness,* how hard they felt things were for them, and these *evil* complaints came up to the ears of the Eternal One. He was furious about this *ingratitude, faithlessness, and lack of vision.* His anger was kindled, and His fire raged among them and devoured some of the camp's perimeter. The people of Israel cried out and ran to Moses and begged him *to do something!* Moses did. He prayed to the Eternal One, and the flames settled down. On account of this incident of the burning fire from the Eternal, the place where it happened is called Taberah, *which means "burning."*

A contingent of Israelites had a strong craving for different food, and the Israelites started complaining again.

Israelites: Who will give us meat to eat? Remember in Egypt when we could eat whatever amount of fish we wanted, or even the abundant cucumbers, melons, leeks, onions, and garlic. *But this, this can hardly be called food at all!* Our appetites have dried up. All we ever have to look at is manna, *manna, manna.*

The thing about the manna is this: It is like coriander seed but the *golden* color of gum resin, falling on the camp with the morning dew. The people could just walk around and pick it up. After grinding it with millstones *to a kind of flour* or crushing it with a mortar, they boiled it in a pot and then formed it into patties. These tasted something like cake prepared with oil, *a kind of sweet bread.* Well, Moses overheard the people in *all* the clans moaning at the door of their tents *about the manna.* The Eternal grew really angry *again,* and Moses thought *the whole situation* was wrong.[28]

Grumbling takes place on the outskirts, behind the scenes or in the shadows, whether it's in your church, your neighborhood, or your workplace. People huddle in the corner, complaining. If you don't want to be one of these people, move to the center of the camp. If you are busy loving and serving others, the last thing you will want to do is complain.

Prayer

God, we thank You for Your inexhaustible grace. Too many times we have deserved Your judgment and punishment. We are so grateful for Your forgiveness. We pray that we will identify our tendency to embrace a complaining spirit as a cancer in the body of Christ. Teach us ways to encourage and lift up our brothers and sisters. If dissatisfaction is the root, plant confidence in us and remind us that through Your Son, Jesus, our relationship is restored. In this growing love and confidence from You, may we bless and encourage one another always. Amen.

EMMANUEL IN HAITI

Emmanuel lives with his mother and three siblings on the Haitian southern coast, near the epicenter of the 2010 earthquake. He helps at home by carrying water, gathering firewood, and caring for animals. He works at home as a subsistence farmer, but soil erosion makes it very difficult to grow crops. Cassava, bananas, and corn are staple foods, but malnutrition is a constant nagging problem. Unclean water causes regular illnesses. Emmanuel likes listening to music and swimming with his friends. Pray that he will be helpful to his mother and siblings, that he will do well in school, and that God will give him good health. Pray that he will help his community develop new methods of sustainable agriculture.

Day 21

M oses's sister Miriam seems to be the perfect big sister. She saved his life when he was a baby, carefully placing him in a basket of reeds and covertly watching over him. Miriam had the remarkable blessing of living to see that same baby lead God's children out of captivity and become the instrument of God's miraculous grace to her people. Can you imagine how blessed she must have felt to sit back and reflect on the ways that God used her obedience? But despite her role in God's rescuing work, Miriam harbored feelings of jealousy against her younger brother. In Numbers 12 we get a unique glimpse of how God deals with jealousy that turns to gossip:

> *While they were at Hazeroth,* Miriam and Aaron chastised Moses for marrying *a foreign woman*—a Cushite (and it was true that he did indeed marry such an African).

Miriam and Aaron: Has the Eternal One spoken only through Moses? *No,* the Eternal has also spoken through us.

Now, the Eternal One heard this. For his part, Moses was a *uniquely* humble fellow, more humble than anyone in the entire world. All of the sudden, the Eternal called *the three siblings together.*

Eternal One: Come here, you three—Moses, Aaron, and Miriam. *Join Me* at the congregation tent.

They did. The Eternal One descended in a cloud-column, stood at the tent opening, and summoned *just* Aaron and Miriam. They came forward.

Eternal One: Listen to Me. When there are prophets in your midst, I, the Eternal One, will show Myself to them in visions, and will sound My voice in their dreams. It's different with My servant, Moses. I have entrusted him above anyone else in My whole house, and with him I communicate face-to-face. We speak directly and without riddles. He can even see the very form of the Eternal. So why aren't you nervous about criticizing My servant, Moses?

The Eternal left, quite angry with Miriam and Aaron. When the cloud lifted from the congregation tent, you could see that Miriam had been stricken with a disfiguring skin condition. Her skin looked white, like snow. Aaron looked at her, saw this, and immediately turned to Moses.

Aaron: Please, Moses, my lord, don't punish us for this offense that we so stupidly committed. Don't leave her in this partial death—like a stillborn baby whose flesh is already half-rotted away!

Moses *(pleading to the Lord)*: O, God, I ask You to please heal her!

Eternal One *(to Moses)*: If her father had *been angry with her and made it obvious by, say,* spitting in her face, wouldn't she have to bear her shame for a week? *Just so,* you must ostracize her from the camp for seven days. After that, she can rejoin the community.[29]

As I reflect on this persistent problem in the life of Miriam and all those with her in the wilderness, I wonder what might have made things different. I know in my life that only prayer, worship, and service have the capacity to turn my bitterness into gratitude.

Can you imagine how different things might have been if all of God's people took the time to worship and pray each morning as they gathered manna? What if someone had suggested that they sing songs and remind one another of God's grace and providence? We need the same remedy. Can we do this when we get in our car, travel to our jobs, lay in our beds at night? What if we are too busy helping people to worry about what others are doing or to think of nasty things to say? What we need is to pray, "God, would You allow me to be so consumed with Your grace that I naturally enter into worship? Would You overwhelm me with Your love so that I can't help but serve people and set aside time to read the Scriptures and play songs that remind me of Your providence?"

Can you set aside extra time for a worshipful reading? You don't need to feel pressure to study the Bible; just read it. Set a time and ask God to show His love for you through it.

The other thing we need is brothers and sisters to speak to us about God. Have you ever started complaining, only to have the person you are speaking with take the ball and carry it that much farther, when what you really needed was help gaining a better perspective? In the next couple of weeks, will you be someone who helps others gain a better perspective? When approached with gossiping or complaining, respond with love: "Is that really how you see it? Have you talked to that person?" It is hard, to be sure, but right. We need to take this seriously. This is the lifeblood of what we do, and our community depends on it.

Jesus said, "Love one another like I have loved you." If all we know is a bunch of facts about God and nothing of His love, we are wasting our time.

Prayer

God, there are days when we can do nothing but sing, jump, shout, and magnify Your name. Times when it is clear that our spirit is energized by You, and our lives are in the flow of Your love. Yet we confess those other days, God, when something different happens—we aren't centered on You, we've let too much time go by without checking in fully, and we've lost direction. It is in these times that we degrade ourselves by making harsh judgments on the people we are supposed to love. God, we need Your help here. Send us a messenger, use our friends to prompt us to make an about-face and mend the gap between our spirit and Your Holy Spirit so that we will again be grateful—thankful for our lives, the things You have both given and taken from us, for ups and downs, but mostly for our closeness to You through the life, death, and resurrection of Your Son, Jesus. Thank You for our daily food. Thank You for clean water. Thank You for surrounding us with friends. Thank You. Amen.

JANET IN UGANDA

Uganda's First Lady, Janet Museveni, approached Living Water International looking for solutions for water-scarce schools in Uganda's southwestern Ruhaama County. "I have been to the schools in Ruhaama," Mrs. Museveni wrote in a letter. "I have seen the empty seats in the classrooms, the children who should be in school walking to collect water that will make them ill." Living Water visited the region and found children with hopes and dreams, and teachers with concerns about declining school attendance. Students were plagued by diseases like cholera, typhoid, dysentery, and hookworm. Many had to walk long distances to collect the water that gave them those diseases. So Uganda's Department of Water and the Environment, Mrs. Museveni, and Living Water International, along with support from dedicated donors, identified fifty Ruhaama County schools in desperate need of water. Now, the seats in the classrooms are beginning to fill up again, with healthy students who are eager to learn. Pray for the schoolchildren of Ruhaama County and the world, that they will no longer have to choose between education and water.

Day 22

How often do you speak of God? How often do you express your gratitude for God's provision, grace, and love to friends and family? Those of us who truly believe that the food we eat, air we breathe, and the undeserved grace that sustains us are gifts from God will speak of our gratitude quite naturally. Many of us were taught to speak about God to others with a planned speech often guided by a tract that attempts to oversimplify the complexities of Christianity and salvation. This has never worked well for me; I end up sounding like a slick infomercial for God, and no one enjoys that. On the other hand, when I learned that I could speak of my doubt, fear, faith, disappointment, and rescue honestly, and often all at once, I found that people loved to hear what I had to say, both privately and publicly.

As we journey with Moses, we see God provide miraculously: God rescued the Israelites from Pharaoh and brought them through perilous dangers sustained only by His hands. And at their camp in a dry land, God brought water from a rock. So imagine with me how Moses might explain all he had experienced when he reunited with his father-in-law, Jethro. A great deal of (miraculous) water had passed under the bridge of God's provision since these two family members had seen one another.

Jethro was a priest among the tribal people in Midian. Midianites did not worship the one true God but rather many gods. Moses met and married Jethro's daughter after fleeing Egypt as a murderer. Moses had two sons, whom he took to Egypt when he returned under God's direction to lead the children of Israel. When things got hard in Egypt, though, he sent his family back to his in-laws while he dealt with two million whiners. The news of God's amazing feats traveled fast, and no doubt Jethro, being a spiritual guide, was eager to investigate the situation with the man who witnessed them firsthand. So Moses took Jethro into his tent to catch up, and of course Moses planned to convince him about the power of the one true God. This is one of those places where I wish I had the whole script instead of just one verse (Exodus 18:8, included below). Imagine how Moses related to Jethro all that had happened to him as they sat together in the tent.

Jethro sent *a servant with* a message for Moses.

Jethro *(to Moses)*: I, Jethro, your father-in-law, am coming out to see you and I'm bringing your wife and two sons with me.

So Moses went out to meet his father-in-law. When he saw him, he bowed down *before Jethro* and kissed him. They each asked how the other was doing, and then they went into Moses' tent.
Moses told Jethro *the whole story. He told him* everything that the Eternal had done to Pharaoh and the Egyptians on behalf of Israel. *He told him* about all the *misery and* tribulations they had run into during their long journey. And *then he told* how the Eternal had rescued them. Jethro was thrilled to hear of all the kindness the Eternal had shown Israel, especially how He rescued them from the *powerful* hand of the Egyptians.

Jethro: Praise to the Eternal, for He rescued you from the powerful hand of the Egyptians, from the cruel grip of Pharaoh. He has liberated His people from beneath the *harsh* hand of their Egyptian *masters.* Now I know *with all my heart* that the Eternal is greater than all gods! Because of the way He delivered His people when Egyptians in their arrogance abused them.[30]

Scripture says Moses didn't hold back any details. We can assume he included his disappointments, fears, and failures as well as each and every miraculous rescue. Many Christians make the tragic mistake of censoring their lives and stories in ways that leave out their dark days. In doing so we become a people who are hard to relate to, and we rob our stories of their redemptive power. My kids were writing stories for their class this past week, and I was trying to explain to my daughter the way conflict is utilized in great storytelling. She wrote a sweet story about going to the zoo and seeing all the animals, and I was telling her, "You need to lose your brother at the zoo or something," and she was horrified.

"That doesn't sound right," she said. "I don't want to lose my brother!"

"But that's what makes the story interesting! That's what makes people sit on the edge of their seats waiting to see what happens. It makes a really good story when he is found at the end, maybe trying to sneak into the lion's habitat." I thought I was pretty convincing, but she liked her story the way it was.

Exodus is a remarkable story, and the way that Moses tells it, both to us and to his father-in-law, leads us to anticipate that the final words will always be "And Yahweh rescued us once again." Have you ever taken the time with close friends or a church small group to sit down and tell your entire story in one sitting? Telling your life story is one of the most remarkable things you can experience. It is good for people to hear it, but it also serves as a reminder to us personally of where we have come from. It is so easy for us to forget the darkest times of our lives, and telling our story reminds us that God is with us.

The first time I went for a body massage, I was assigned to a woman who believed deeply in Native American spirituality. As she began the massage she asked me what I did for a living, and I let her know I was a pastor. She was curious how a young, scruffy hooligan with infinite knots in his back could be in this line of work. She had an insatiable appetite for spiritual truth, and for every minute of my therapy she peppered me with questions:

"How do you know God exists?"
"How do you know that Jesus is the only way to salvation?"
"How do you see Jesus change lives?"
"How do you like the pressure?"

140

I told her all I knew about God. At the end, she didn't charge me for the massage and asked if I could come back next week and tell her more about God. This went on for about a month before she came to faith and we baptized her and two of her sons. I believe the reason she came so quickly to faith in God was because she was already deeply spiritual. Much like Jethro, a priest who had not yet heard the stories of the one true God. Do you know anyone like Jethro? Someone who is very spiritual but doesn't believe in Jesus yet? They are already searching for divinity or sense something greater, but maybe Christianity has never been communicated clearly to them. Are you the person they have been waiting for? Tell them your story!

Prayer

God, we thank You that the dark times in our lives are a living testimony to Your love, grace, and deliverance. Give us the faith to share the whole story of the ways that You have saved us. Like Moses, who not only spoke of his great triumphs but also of his miserable failures. Lead us by Your Spirit to those who need to hear, and as You did with Moses, who was so often afraid to speak, give us the words. Amen.

AAILYAH IN KENYA

Aailyah lives with her parents in a small village in central Kenya. She helps out at home by carrying water, which is a part of daily survival in a climate that is mostly dry. Both of her parents find part-time work as common laborers, so they can try to provide the corn, beans, milk, and beef that are part of the staple diet in their area. As part of Compassion's ministry, Aailyah participates in church activities and likes playing with her friends. Pray that God will protect Aailyah and her family from drought and famine, and that she will learn how precious she is as a child of God.

FEAST DAY: Celebrating God

In the Old Testament, God specifically commands that His people celebrate.

The Eternal One spoke to Moses *regarding the holy days.*

Eternal One: *Go,* talk to the Israelites. Tell them that I have appointed *certain* feasts to be celebrated. You are to *honor these times and* declare them as sacred assemblies.

You have six days to do your ordinary work; but when the seventh day arrives, it is a Sabbath and must be a day of complete rest, a time for sacred assembly. No work is allowed. Wherever you live, celebrate the Sabbath in My honor.

Here are times I have appointed for sacred assemblies; you are to *celebrate these feasts and* declare them *publicly* at their appointed times. *In the spring* on the fourteenth day of the first month, My Passover begins at first light. When the fifteenth day arrives, you are to celebrate the Feast of Unleavened Bread in My honor.

For the next seven days, the only bread you are allowed to eat is unleavened bread. On the first day *of the feast,* I want you to gather for a sacred assembly; you are not allowed to do any ordinary work. On each of the seven days *of the feast,* present a fire-offering to Me. When the seventh day arrives, hold a sacred assembly; you are not allowed to do any ordinary work.[31]

Have you ever taken the time to consider how often God commands His people to celebrate?

- Rosh Hashanah (New Year)—a time of introspection and celebration that God is sovereign
- Yom Kippur (Day of Atonement)—a day of fasting to acknowledge our mistakes and pray for forgiveness
- Sukkot (Festival of Booths)—a day devoted to eating and sleeping and a reminder of God's love and protection
- Shemini Atzeret/Simchat Torah—a celebration of the gift of having a Torah-inspired life
- Pesach (Passover)—a celebration of the exodus from Egyptian slavery and true spiritual freedom
- Shavuot (Festival of Weeks)—a celebration of the Torah coming to God's people at Mount Sinai

God is serious when it comes to setting aside time to celebrate. Do you think it is possible to celebrate God's love too much? On the other hand, is it possible to celebrate His love too little? I think so. If we err, we likely err by not celebrating God enough.

So take these feasting days and do something special. As you eat great food, take a special trip, dance, and laugh, do it as unto the Lord.

Prayer

God, You have blessed us in immeasurable ways. May we see You today past our plates into all areas of our life. May we celebrate through movement, art, and embraces—may we celebrate to Your delight. Amen.

JANVIER IN HAITI

Janvier lives with his parents and three siblings on the Haitian island of La Gonave. His mother and father are both teachers, and Janvier helps out at home by carrying water, mending clothes, and cleaning. Beans, fish, and rice are part of the family's everyday diet, but clean water is a problem. Eighty percent of the people in the community are unemployed, and there are few options for people to find better jobs on the island. Janvier enjoys playing soccer, telling stories, and reading, and is involved at his church. Please pray that he will study well and value education, as his parents do. Pray that he will trust God to meet his needs, and that God will protect him from sickness.

Day 23

If I had the money I'd hire a PR firm to help rebrand the Ten Commandments in the marketplace. In some corners of our world they are despised. Christians and non-Christians fight one another over whether they should be displayed in public spaces while others accept them as innocuous moral standards that should be accepted by all cultures and people. When you ask most people to describe the Big 10 (not the football conference), they describe them as rules to live by. You are probably familiar with the Ten Commandments as "the ten things you should never ever (ever) do." But they are hardly that. Not at all.

In my experience rules don't take us very far, and these commands, when we truly hear them, do much more than restrict our behavior. Too often what has been portrayed is that faith in Jesus is about obeying these ten rules plus a few we have added along the way, most often related to alcohol, sex, and tobacco. Christianity, then, as a religion becomes just a behavior modification system, and behavior modification systems don't work. They are a waste of time. Don't believe me? Next January 1, make a resolution to lose fifteen pounds and keep them off. Willing ourselves to do something is very different from actually doing it.

In eighth grade, my friend Chris and I were inseparable. One Christmas we both got bows and arrows, which for a young teenaged boy is one of the coolest gifts. Behind his house we'd shoot at targets, which is hard and takes a long time to master. But one day, his mother laid down a rule: "Boys, you can shoot those things as much as you want, but there will be no flaming arrows." All of the sudden, shooting flaming arrows became the obsession of two young boys. In that moment it became clear to both of us that we would accomplish nothing until we shot flaming arrows. Consequently, we almost burned down all of Texas.

If she had never brought it up, we may never have thought of it. This is what rules do: they taunt you to break them. They have the potential to bring out the worst in us, not the best.

I am convinced that Exodus 20 is the most misunderstood passage in all of Scripture, because as you will see, the Ten Commandments are much more than a set of rules.

The first two commandments in many ways summarize the following eight; if you keep the first two, the others will easily fall into place; if you do not, nothing else will matter. As God's people were struggling to find their way in the wilderness, God stepped in with truths intended to deliver them all.

Then God began to speak *directly to all the people.*

Eternal One: I am the Eternal, your God. I led you out of Egypt and liberated you from lives of slavery *and oppression.*

You are not to serve any other gods before Me.

You are not to make any idol *or image of other gods. In fact,* you are not to make an image of anything in the heavens above, on the earth below, or in the waters beneath. You are not to bow down and serve any image, for I the Eternal your God am a jealous God. As for those who are not loyal to Me, their children will endure the consequences of their sins for three or four generations. But for those who love Me and keep My directives, their children will experience My loyal love for a thousand generations.[32]

When God says He is laying down the law, we naturally think, "Here it comes. These are the rules, this is what I must abide by." But the commandments are not about external actions but about issues of the heart, and they all flow from these two commands. Because here's the trouble: you can do the right thing, but if you do it for the wrong reasons you are in more trouble than if you just did the wrong thing. The motivation is wrong even though the action may be right, and if the motivation is wrong, there has not been a heart change. These commands are not written so we can

146

measure ourselves against one another; they are purposeful in the development of our relationship to the Creator. We don't need to post them on a wall or fight over them; they are something that is written on our hearts to remind us of the importance of our relationship with our heavenly Father. The commandments are about building a life on the foundation of Christ and what God has put in us, the Holy Spirit, and expanding that love to the people and places around us.

The beauty of spending time on these two commands is that we begin to realize that our sin is not merely about our actions but about what we love. For instance, if you are a parent, you may find that one moment your love for your child is a beautiful thing, and then all of a sudden this switch flips and your child becomes the object of your affection and focus instead of the God who gave you this child. If your focus is on your children and not on God, your children can easily become an idol. Which is not good for them or for you; it is destructive. Have no other gods before Me—that means anything that becomes more important than God. Paul talks about this clearly in Colossians 3. Try to hear these words with your heart.

So *it comes down to this:* since you have been raised with the Anointed One, *the Liberating King,* set your mind on heaven above. The Anointer is there, seated at God's right hand. Stay focused on what's above, not on earthly things, because your *old* life is dead and gone. Your *new* life is now hidden, enmeshed with the Anointed who is in God. On that day when the Anointed One—who is our very life—is revealed, you will be revealed with Him in glory! So kill your earthly impulses: loose sex, impure actions, unbridled sensuality, wicked thoughts, and greed (which is *essentially* idolatry). It's because of these that God's wrath is coming [upon the sons and daughters of disobedience], *so avoid them at all costs.* These are the same things you once pursued, and together you spawned a life of evil. But now make sure you shed such things: anger, rage, spite, slander, and abusive language. And don't go on lying to each other since you have sloughed away your old skin along with its evil practices for a fresh new you, which is continually renewed in knowledge according to the image of the One who created you. In this re-creation there is no distinction between Greek and Jew, circumcised and uncircumcised, barbarian and conqueror, or slave and free because the Anointed is the whole and dwells in us all.

Since you are all set apart by God, made holy and dearly loved, clothe yourselves with *a holy way of life*: compassion, kindness, humility, gentleness, and patience. Put up with one another. Forgive. Pardon any offenses against one another, as the Lord has pardoned you, because you should act in kind. But above all these, put on love! Love is the perfect tie to bind these together. Let your hearts fall under the rule of the Anointed's peace (the peace you were called to as one body), and be thankful.[33]

How do we change? Focus on heavenly things. On Jesus. Stay focused on what's above. Do everything in the name of Jesus. If you take Jesus out of Christianity, you will have nothing but a set of rules. You will be like me with the flaming arrows, wondering how fast the flames are going to grow. Jesus changes our hearts, and without heart change, behavior change is meaningless. We will fail. Failure is painful but it is also instructive. I hope for our sake we learn along the way. The proof of our faith is not in willing ourselves to do the right thing, it is in allowing Jesus to capture our hearts. When He does, we root out the other things, and our hearts can sing.

Prayer

Thank You, Father, that You have written these words on our hearts, the most tender of spaces, the organ that pumps life throughout our body. Let these words remind us when our life's direction has turned from Your business and a right relationship with you. Lord, reveal to us what we have allowed into Your space. Show us what we have loved more than You so we have the opportunity to put those things in their right place and come closer to You. Amen.

GUDIA IN INDIA

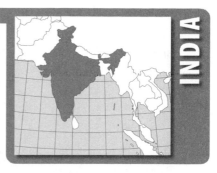

Gudia lives with her father, mother, and two siblings in India. She likes playing house and playing with simple dolls. Her father finds part-time work as an unskilled laborer, and her mother stays home. Fish, rice, potatoes, and chicken are part of the normal diet, but there is often not enough food to go around. Water has to be carried from wells far away. Alcoholism and drug addiction are major problems, and local church leaders report that child molestation is common. Pray that as Gudia grows up, her family will be loving and peaceful. Pray that she will be protected from major illness, and that she will become a woman who sets an example for other girls in the community.

Day 24

I believe the next command, like the first, is a window through which we understand all the rest of the commands. This command has the power to change our lives, because our lives are oriented around comparison.

> You are not to covet what your neighbor has or set your heart on getting his house, his wife, his male or female servants, his ox or donkey, or anything else that belongs to your neighbor.[34]

This urge to compare starts for most of us at a very young age. We create a pecking order in almost every context and evaluate who is better than us, or less than. Remember junior high when you'd rank in your notebook which classmates were popular or not? As adults we are more discreet, but old habits die hard. What criteria do you use to create your rankings? Fashion. Power. Money. Beauty. Charisma. Education. Vocation.

I don't know when you first realized that your life was being measured, compared, and evaluated based on the people around you. I have a very vivid memory from the first grade, when a classmate began to clearly explain to me where I was in the pecking order of our class because instead of having an alligator on my shirt, I had a fire-breathing dragon. Much of life is spent looking at what others have and using their standing to see how we measure up. This is coveting.

A cultural debate is raging because Amy Chua, a self-described "Tiger Mom," believes most of today's children have been coddled and rewarded despite the fact that they have not accomplished anything. To her, self-esteem should be rooted in accomplishments, while other moms say accomplishments must be rooted in self-esteem. Both views miss the mark, in my opinion. This is one of the many places where a biblical worldview defies the wisdom of the world.

The Scriptures declare that my value comes from my Creator, not from my love of self or accomplishments.

> For You shaped me, inside *and out*.
> You knitted me together in my mother's womb *long before I took my first breath*.[35]

When the actions of our lives are motivated by this truth, we can finally breathe. Can you imagine a life without the continual comparison to one another? When we begin to take God at His word, and as we become truly thankful for our daily bread, we are freed from the notion that those who have more are more than and those who have less are less than. We no longer need to elevate or lower ourselves but can see others as equals—people who are created in God's image, equally broken in search of the way.

What God is calling us to is to live focused on Jesus. Not on obsessions or cravings of the moment, but Jesus—only Jesus. Of course, no matter how clear our focus is today, tomorrow it can get fuzzy. We build up idols. Our idols are rarely primitive deities; most often our hearts are captured by stuff that we or our neighbors have acquired.

Jesus: You know that *Hebrew Scripture* sets this standard *of justice and punishment*: take an eye for an eye and a tooth for a tooth. But I say this: don't fight against the one who is working evil against you. If someone strikes you on the right cheek, you are to turn and offer him your left cheek. If someone connives to get your shirt, give him your jacket as well. If someone forces you to walk with him for a mile, walk with him for two instead. If someone asks you for something, give it to him. If someone wants to borrow something from you, do not turn away.

You have been taught to love your neighbor and hate your enemy. But I tell you this: love your enemies. Pray for those who torment you and persecute you— in so doing, you become children of your Father in heaven. He, after all, loves each of us—good and evil, kind and cruel. He causes the sun to rise *and shine* on evil and good alike. He causes the rain *to water the fields* of the righteous and *the fields* of the sinner. It is easy to love those who love you—even a tax collector can love those who love him. And it is easy to greet your friends—even outsiders do that! *But you are called to something higher:* "Be perfect, as your Father in heaven is perfect."[36]

We would love to sprinkle a little Christianity, a little truth, a little moral teaching on top of some Old Testament law and live out an eye for an eye, but Jesus changes everything. The life the gospel is calling us to is a radically generous life. You want my coat? Ah, just take it all. We have to take the words of Jesus seriously not only in our study and reflection but also in our actions. God is calling us to something more beautiful than just loving the people who are easy to love.

Paul says:

> I could hardly contain my joy in the Lord when I realized you have started to show your care for me once again. Since you have not had the opportunity to show how much you cared until now, *I want you to know how it touched me.* I am not saying this because I am in need. I have learned to be content in whatever circumstances. I know how to survive in tight situations, and I know how to enjoy having plenty. In fact, I have learned how to face any circumstances: fed or hungry, with or without. I can be content in any and every situation through the Anointed One who is my power and strength.[37]

Paul takes us back to the first command. When Jesus is at the center for me, I can be content with whatever He gives me. He could give me much, He could give me little; I could be hungry, I could be well fed; I could be at perfect peace with my neighbor, I could be in conflict; but as I abide in Jesus I find a contentment that flows into all that I am.

I believe that when we as a people focus on Jesus and rest in the contentment of what He's blessed us with, we become a different people. When our attention is fixed on Jesus, when our life is about a right relationship with our Creator, the daily struggle to prove ourselves falls to the wayside.

Prayer

Thank You, Lord, for the sacrificial act of Your Son, Jesus. This one act, Father, is more than enough, yet we continue to fall, we continue to strive in wrong directions. Your command is clear: don't desire what others have. Reset our hearts, Lord, and align our vision with Yours. Show us how to build our lives on the foundation You have established within us, that we would clearly see Your provision and not be afraid. Help us to love one another, even where there is discord. Help us to be brave and have conversations that are hard with people we normally would try to measure our lives against. Help us to see ourselves and others through Your love; help us to be the type of people who respond to hate with love.

May the world notice that we live like Paul, completely content in feast or famine. May they encounter You by the way we live our lives. Amen.

ADI IN INDONESIA

Adi lives with his father, mother, and two siblings in Indonesia. Neither of his parents works full-time outside the home, but they find work as common laborers when they can, and try to grow food to eat right where they live. Adi helps out by caring for the other children, making beds, and running errands. Their main food is rice. Adi is an average student who likes art, singing, and playing with cars. Pray that through the local church where he receives help from Compassion, he will find the assistance he needs to develop his potential as a good student. Pray that he will develop a relationship with Jesus that will bring deep hope to his family and community.

Day 25

In looking at the Ten Commandments given to Moses in Exodus 20, we find they are more about the heart than about establishing rules. Following God is more than willing ourselves to do things. With that said, there are some behaviors that are particularly destructive in any and every community. God wants to be clear with us about each of these.

Don't murder. Before you skip to the next command in confidence that you are unlikely or incapable of taking someone's life, let's look at the deeper issues. Do we treat human life with respect? As we read the Gospels, it becomes clear that Jesus values every human being. No one is unimportant to God. The children, outsiders, criminals, adulterers, the lowly, and the unborn are all part of God's chosen family. We must live in a way that honors the value God places on every human being, no matter his or her age, history, mistakes, race, creed, or status. May we become truly faithful to this command in every part of our lives.

Don't commit adultery. God in all His full, beautiful imagination made us both spiritual and sexual beings. He wants us to preserve the gift of intimate sexual acts for the remarkable union of marriage. He wants husband and wife to come together and in that fidelity find hope, trust, and beauty. This marker of Christian marriage is a symbol of our fidelity to God. This command is quite clear. Many do not like this command; they do not believe it is culturally relevant. Stay faithful anyway. It will serve you well.

Don't steal. Do not take what is not yours. This is the same in stores as it is in the corporate setting, even with intellectual ideas. Integrity matters to God. The truth is that anything we wrongly acquire will not be a blessing; it will be a curse.

Don't bear false witness. Do not lie about your neighbor. Tell the truth whether or not it is expedient. Our culture has become so soft on truth that we are able to deceive, misdirect, beguile, and quite literally con others, feeling all the while as though we have never actually lied. The world is longing for people who will tell the truth. One of the great marks of true Christianity is a community of people who do what they say they will do, and can be trusted. In the long run, truth tellers will experience the kind of joy and success that can never be found on the path of dishonesty.

Prayer

God, it is clear that You value every life. You have breathed into all of us the life that we so easily take for granted. It is a testimony to Your incredible imagination and desire that we are all unique. Help us to be obedient to Your basic directions of engagement, of care for the gift of life. We live as part of Your great family. May our actions bring unity, joy, and prosperity to our brothers and sisters both near and far. Amen.

YAKEMIS IN COLOMBIA

Yakemis lives in Colombia with her parents. She helps out around her home by washing clothes, helping in the kitchen, and cleaning. Her father doesn't have a full-time job, and her mother works part-time at church. Yakemis is an above-average student with musical talent, and is regularly involved with the youth group at her church. The main diet for people in Yakemis's community is rice, corn, and bananas, but poor nutrition is often an issue because of high unemployment. Please pray that Yakemis's faith will grow and that her family will continue to trust God to meet all their needs.

Day 26

Everyone is longing for the good life. While self-help books gush guarantees of happiness, the Scriptures offer very few of them, and guarantees are especially sparse in the Ten Commandments. But today we will look at one.

Question: which command do you think offers hope for the future? It might be the one we focus on the least.

Eternal One: *You are to* honor your father and mother. If you do, you *and your children* will live long *and well* in the land the Eternal your God *has promised to* give you.[38]

When our lives, actions, and attitudes seek to bring honor to our parents, we can expect to live long and well. It is fascinating that the commandments do not focus merely on moral action and idolatry. They call us into a deeper love for God and involve us in the story of our parents and grandparents. In our culture we emphasize individualism almost to the point that many of us have lost any sense of story, belonging, and heritage. This commandment is given not only to young children but to all of us—whether our parents are living or not.

There is a reason why so much of the hard work people have to do in counseling is related to coming to terms with their parents. If you have anger, bitterness, and unresolved issues with your parents, it is hard to discern how your life and actions honor them, which makes it hard to live well. One thing that has been clear to me through the years is that my parents have been easier to honor than many of the parents of my peers. In short, my parents are honorable.

I watch friends as they enter periods of doubt, where they question whether or not God truly loves them. This kind of struggle is heart wrenching and paralyzing. One possible source of this (not the only one) is having grown up with irresponsible or unloving parents. I have all kinds of doubt in my life, but I don't ever recall doubting the love of God. I doubt whether I will love God in return. I doubt whether I will be faithful. I doubt the reasons God has to allow this or that. But I don't doubt the love of God, and I attribute that sense of deep and profound love to my bond with my earthly parents. In the Old Testament a bond was called a covenant; I understand it today to be the true and unconditional love of the heavenly Father.

The apostle Paul underscores this command in his letter to the Ephesians.

> *Now to you,* children, obey your parents in the Lord because this is right *in God's eyes.* This is the first commandment onto which He added a promise: "Honor your father and your mother, and if you do, you will live long and well in this land.
>
> And, fathers, do not drive your children mad, but nurture them in the discipline and teaching *that comes* from the Lord.[39]

Isn't it interesting that Paul speaks specifically to fathers? The loving discipline of a tender father can make a world of difference in the life of a child. We all know children who don't obey their parents, and they are a challenge to be around. Paul reminds us that children are to obey their parents, but also that fathers are to discipline children from a loving parental bond. He says not to exasperate them or push them away. How would the world be different if every child was disciplined by a father in the context of a deep and profound love?

If you are a parent, make sure to solidify the bond of unconditional love with your children. Express to them your love and find ways to show it. If your parents are still living, make sure to show them honor. Some parents are more honorable than others, but we must learn what it means to give them honor and accept the legacy we have been given. Sometimes that legacy is one of pain, abuse, and suffering; but we can seek redemption and honor in even the worst scenarios. It is never easy, but redemption is always a better path than anger. This would have been understood more clearly in the Eastern context of the Hebrews; in the West we think very little about honor being passed down through generations. But let's be clear: our lack of focus and clarity about this command can often be a great source of trouble in our lives.

Prayer

God, we often forget that You made us a people of heritage. Our bodies are designed by the characteristics of our parents, and brought to life by Your breath. You sent a model for the good life—Jesus the Christ. He is more than a guide; He is a brother. Through His death, we are restored to You, our heavenly Father, and we are so thankful. Help us, Father, to live lives that honor our parents and any person who has helped bring us to our current place in life. Some of us are experiencing discord in our parent-child relationships and need healing. Help us to step into Your presence; bring to our awareness the places we harbor bitterness and pain; heal our hearts. Help us to be reminded of Your great love so that from this place of restoration, we can bring our children near to us and point them to You. Amen.

A WOMAN IN GUATEMALA

The kids were from Guatemala's highlands, so they had never seen anything like this. The crew from Living Water International's short-term trip developed their new well, injecting it with compressed air, blasting water out to clean it. Kids lined up to be pummeled by the gushing water, giggling, clean, and giddy. A single Guatemalan woman, quiet, colorful in Mayan garb, approached the well, and there among the children's laughter, cupped her hand and gathered water that dribbled down a length of casing. She tasted and without ever making eye contact with the American crew, she dropped to her knees, pulled a length of woven cloth over her head for privacy, and prayed. "She sees," whispered Jaime, the leader of the drilling crew, to his boss. "She knows." Jaime was referring to Isaiah 41:17–20: "The poor and needy search for water. . . . I the LORD will answer them . . . so that people may see and know . . . the hand of the LORD has done this." Please pray that all who thirst would see and know what the Guatemalan woman experienced at the well.

Day 27

Our natural tendency in life and faith is to try to make things as simple as possible. Mystery and tension can be a challenge. For this reason we can end up reducing these ten lessons, these ten important concepts in Exodus, into a checklist. This allows us to feel a sense of accomplishment because "I have not violated that rule." When this happens we are creeping into the territory of the rich young ruler. (Jesus, remember, said that if the ruler had mastered all the commandments, to then sell everything, give the money to the poor and follow Him.) So before you assume you understand this next command, ask God to give you some new insight.

Eternal One: You are not to use My name for *your own* idle purposes, for the Eternal will punish anyone who treats His name as anything less than sacred.[40]

Too often this command has been summed up like this: do not say God's name as a profanity. We insert "gosh" and assume we have taken the high road. Jews have taken this command to mean they are not to speak or write the name of God—period. As you might expect, this command is much more complex and heartfelt than either of these interpretations would suggest. In the Hebrew it would be better understood to mean the following: do not carry or embody God's name in a way that empties or belittles it.

There are a million ways to do this, of course, and most of them involve our pride. We forget God's grace, love, care, and His miraculous rescue that comes to us time and again. Keeping this in mind, we might be better served if we shift our focus from what we are not to do and contemplate what we are to do. We are to revere God and worship Him. This is one of the reasons we gather with local believers on a weekly basis. When we gather in one place and voice prayers and read the Scriptures and sing songs of His grace, our hearts are filled again with the glory, beauty, and grandeur of God.

Instead of belittling or otherwise misusing the name of God by employing it to justify our purposes, we should fill up on the grandeur, beauty, and glory of God. Find times and places where you reconnect with the glory of God. For you, for instance, this might happen at the beach or elsewhere in nature. Wherever it is, do the work of regularly filling up on the grandeur of God. When we do this well, we will be much less prone to misusing His name.

Prayer

God, we are amazed that You, the very Creator of the universe, chose to draw near to us and reveal Your name to us. We live in the blessing of Your grace and authority. Forgive us when we undermine Your work in the world by pursuing our idle purposes. May we sense more than ever Your glory and grace over our choices, actions, and relationships, so that we would be bright reflections of Your name and nature. Amen.

MARCUS IN NICARAGUA

Marcus lives with his mother and one sibling in central Nicaragua. His mother works part-time, and Marcus helps her around the house by running errands and cleaning. Their daily meals include corn, beans, bread, and rice. Marcus is a bright student who likes to play soccer with his friends, and he stays involved at his church. Drugs, alcoholism, and gang activity are common in his community. Pray that Marcus will find good role models at his church and resist the pressure to get involved in crime as he grows older. Pray that his mother will have good health and will understand God's deep love for her.

Day 28

I can thrive in chaos. When energy is moving and creative juices are flowing, I am in my element. I am known to book a trip last minute and hop on a plane to any time zone in the world if there is something that needs to be done. However, if I don't put my car keys in the very same place every time I travel, they will be lost. These routines, even for those of us who are a bit anarchist in the way we live, are stabilizing and important to build into our daily lives, lest the business of life overrun us and we lose focus on what is truly meaningful.

If it weren't important to rest, God wouldn't have done it and certainly wouldn't have put it in the Scriptures as a command. Resting builds up our mental, physical, and spiritual foundation; it changes the way we live and the choices we make. This command may not seem as clear an imperative as "You shall not murder," but it may be the founding idea that keeps you in a place of health.

Eternal One: *You and your family are to* remember the Sabbath day; *set it apart,* and keep it holy. You have six days to do all your work, but the seventh day is *to be different; it is* the Sabbath of the Eternal your God. *Keep it holy* by not doing any work—not you, your sons, your daughters, your male and female servants, your livestock, or any outsiders living among you. For the Eternal made the heavens *above,* the earth *below,* the seas, and all the creatures in them in six days. Then, on the seventh day, He rested. That is why He blessed the Sabbath Day and made it sacred.[41]

Take a minute to remember what this past week felt like. How quickly have you been moving? Do you have a tendency, like I do, to drive three to four miles per hour over the speed limit? I am in a hurry. I have places to go and important things to do. I often push the limits of my physical capacity rather than resting and arriving somewhere at peace. Do you feel pushed to the limit?

There is something to learn from our pace. Contemplate the pace at which you walk. Now imagine walking in your neighborhood. If you walk too fast, you may not see the people around you, but if you slow your pace down a bit, you will start to see what God is doing in the world. What if you simply paused every once in a while?

Our problem is not one of comprehension. We understand what the command means. God says quite clearly we are to honor the Sabbath. The Shabbat. The sacred day set apart. Make sure it remains holy. Work hard six days, one day off. Do all of your work in six days and then on the seventh day, remove yourself from emails, work, phones, and texts . . . and just allow yourself to be in the presence of God.

I am not one who always does this well. But I know God has called me to continue to build Sabbath into my life. I see my effectiveness peak when I do it and waver when I don't.

You don't have to be a person of faith to understand this truth. I recently had a conversation with the contractor repairing my roof. He explained that his crew needed to work over the weekend. "I'm curious," I said to him. "Do you normally work on Sunday?" He said, "No, we don't typically work on Sunday, but my guys are rested from the rain. Normally, if my guys don't have that day off, they aren't rested, which means they're in danger. If they get on the roof without rest, they're much more likely to fall or make simple mistakes they wouldn't make otherwise." Now, this guy wasn't a believer, but he understands Sabbath. If you don't rest, you are headed for a fall.

You may not work on a roof, but don't be fooled: your rest matters. God's command is very clear. Work six days. Work really hard. And the seventh day: rest. The seventh day is for Yahweh.

Prayer

God, we are so thankful that at the end of a hard week's work, You call us to rest with You. May the blessing of the Sabbath be present in our daily decisions. May we build our lives around this solid foundation of presence with You. Help us to notice when we are out of rest. Give us the courage to open up a space in our daily and weekly routines to renew our covenant love with You. Fortify us in these times together, Father, to reenter the world as mindful citizens of Your kingdom. Amen.

LUIS IN PERU

Luis lives with his father and his mother near Lima, Peru. He helps out at home by washing clothes and cleaning, but his father does not have a full-time job, and this can make family life difficult. Corn, beans, and chicken are staple foods for Luis. Poor community sanitation is a major source of health problems in the area. There is no trash service, so garbage pollutes the river, and stomach ailments and skin infections are common. Pray that Luis will trust in Jesus and will learn to care for his environment and understand how to help his community live in health and peace.

Celebrating the Sabbath

Sabbath is a principle to be lived out, not a rule that must be kept. But understanding Sabbath outside of a legalistic perspective does not make it any less important. Depending on your vocation, keeping the Sabbath can be a very challenging practice to integrate into your life. The world we live in is so fast paced, and it seems that every industry believes it has to deliver products and services at the whim of customers.

Decades ago the world slowed down on Sundays. Yes, doctors and nurses were ready to help in case of an emergency, but otherwise the world seemed to stop. That is no longer the case, so those who practice spiritual rest are forced to be creative and resourceful. They must display tremendous dedication to nurture this spiritual practice.

This is one of the most challenging and important spiritual practices to integrate well in the life of a pastor. Pastors are called to work so that others can seek rest and worship, but if we do not have time set aside for our own rest, worship, and sacred feasting, we will career off the path quickly. Following are some of the formidable foes I face in trying to keep the Sabbath well. Do they resonate with you?

1. **Swimming upstream.** We need to find a way to keep the Sabbath when everyone else is working. This requires extreme

discipline and a commitment to having sacred space set aside in our week.

2. **Growing families.** If you have children, you may find that the rhythms that worked well in one season will not necessarily work in the next. For instance, when my kids were homeschooled, we had tremendous flexibility. As their lives and schedules fill with musicals, practices, school, co-ops, Bible studies, birthday parties, and sports, setting aside time for Sabbath rest becomes increasingly difficult.

3. **Growing churches or vocational responsibilities.** As our churches, companies, or organizations grow, so do our responsibilities. When we started Ecclesia, I was preaching one service on Sunday evening. Now I preach four on Sunday and one on Saturday night; it changes everything.

As a pastor, I try to wrap myself in Sabbath on both sides of our weekend worship services. On the front end I seek time with the family, and on the back end I seek time alone. If I do this well, I am ready for work again on Tuesday morning. If I do not, I go into the week on a major deficit that I am constantly trying to conquer.

Your life may look entirely different than mine. But it will still require the same kind of creativity and dedication if you are going to follow this command. Are you willing to experiment with ways to create space for prayer, worship, rest, and a sense of sacredness in your life? Where can you start?

Prayer

God, we thank You for instructing us in immensely practical ways. We are a people made to work hard and to rest well. Our bodies and spirits are suffering because we have ignored this command. Forgive us. Give us insight as we find new ways of resting weekly in Your presence. Amen.

MANZENI IN UGANDA

Manzeni lives with her grandparents and three other children in a village in Uganda. Her grandparents both work as farmers, but poor farmland, lack of good drinking water, and limited resources make life difficult. Manzeni's family lives in a mud home with a dirt floor. Corn and beans make up the bulk of their diet. Malaria, respiratory infections, and dysentery are common. Even though Manzeni lives in desperate conditions, she likes singing and telling stories. She attends church regularly and sings in the choir. Pray that God will give Manzeni's grandparents strength and health, and that Manzeni will grow up to change her community.

Day 29

Ever leave your house, start driving, and then completely forget where you are going? Or worse, have you ever arrived somewhere and had no memory of how you got there? I have been on my way to a meeting only to realize that I left my house in my gym clothes.

My favorite television series, *Lost*, was a hit not just because of brilliant writing, a remarkably beautiful group of castaways, and a treasure trove of religious and philosophical insight. Viewers connected to it on a very basic level because we all know what it feels like to be lost. I have some horror stories from my days before GPS, but they all pale in comparison to God's children running in circles through a very small area for 40 years.

We, like God's children, too often lose sight of our destination. We must remember that our journey, including our current 40-day journey, is leading us to a land of milk and honey. We are leaving behind oppression, slavery, and a life devoted to an empire in Egypt and exchanging it for a land of abundance. As a non-agrarian people, we may not fully understand the meaning of the "land of milk and honey," but it is what we long for whether we realize it or not. The Hebrew words tell us the Promised Land is a fertile land, flowing or gushing with both milk and honey. Think volcanoes bubbling up with honey. You don't have to be Winnie the Pooh to realize that flowing honey is a strikingly appetizing image. But we have to look past the honey to understand the meaning.

What do bees and honey represent in the environment? A strong bee population signals a fruitful land. One of the problems we have in our land is a lack of bees. We had a big hullabaloo at our house a year ago because a family of bees decided to nest in the overhang of our roof. The nest was located in a very tough place to get to, and I could not find someone to remove it carefully. The only people willing to remedy my problem would do so by exterminating the bees. I refused, because the United States is facing a devastating shortage of bees.

Bees are essential for agriculture and the pollination of crops. Bees represent a land of blooming flowers where fruit and vegetables are growing aplenty. Honey represents a balanced and beautiful environment.

Today I want us to meditate together on this land of milk and honey. For us it doesn't mean we are going to a physical location; it is about letting this land of abundance collide with our world. Jesus called it the kingdom of God.

Let us begin by wrestling with a question similar to the one Jesus asked the crippled man at the pool of Bethesda: do you want to go to this land of beauty and shalom?

In Jerusalem they came upon a pool by the sheep gate surrounded by five covered porches. In Hebrew this place is called Bethesda.

Crowds of people lined the area, lying around the porches. All of these people were *disabled in some way;* some were blind, lame, paralyzed, or plagued by diseases, and they were waiting for the waters to move. From time to time, a heavenly messenger would come to stir the water in the pool. Whoever reached the water first and got in after it was agitated would be healed of his or her disease. In the crowd, Jesus noticed one particular man who had been living with his disability for 38 years. He knew this man had been waiting here a long time.

Jesus (to the disabled man): Are you *here in this place* hoping to be healed?

Disabled Man: Kind Sir, I wait, *like all of these people,* for the waters to stir; *but I cannot walk. If I am to be healed in the waters,* someone must carry me into the pool. Without a helping hand, someone else beats me to the water's edge each time it is stirred.

Jesus: Stand up, carry your mat, and walk.

At the moment Jesus uttered these words, a healing energy coursed through the man and returned life to his limbs—he stood and walked *for the first time in 38 years.* But this was the Sabbath Day; *and any work, including carrying a mat, was prohibited on this day.*[42]

As we enter into the final weeks on this pilgrimage through the wilderness, we too encounter these questions: Do you want to be healed? Do you want to find your comforts in the temporary pleasures of this world? Do you want to find your security in your bank account? Are you leaving the wilderness for a land of promise or will you return to the chains of Egypt?

Prayer

God, as we walk in circles, as we swarm about like bees seeking a place to nest, we consider all that You have done for us. More and more as we walk, we are understanding what it means to be free, to find our joy in things that cannot be bought and sold. We catch glimpses as a community of Your love when we lean on one another, listen and engage in life stories, and remind one another that we are children of hope. Children of grace. Children of love. We know You embrace us in one another's arms. Though we can still feel the cutting of the shackles around our ankles, we also feel the warmth of the sun healing our wounds. God, we thank You that You are near. We thank You for reminding us through our brothers and sisters that though we are vulnerable in the wilderness, You are solidifying Your plans for our deliverance. Help us to choose it. Help us, Lord. Amen.

SAMUEL IN COLOMBIA

Samuel lives with his mother and three siblings in Colombia. In his community, poverty and unemployment mean that drug use, family violence, and alcoholism are common. Samuel's mother does not have a full-time job, so they rely on help from their neighbors, church, and Compassion sponsorship. Beans, corn, and bananas are the most common foods Samuel and his family eat. Samuel enjoys running and playing soccer and attending Bible classes at church. Please pray that his mother will find regular work and that as Samuel grows he will break the cycle of poverty in his family.

Day 30

Do you remember a particular moment in your life when you felt a deep connection to God? A time when you were dialed in to His voice? For most of us, these times have come when we were soaking in the beauty of creation: prayerful walks on the beach, a retreat in the woods, hiking a majestic mountain, or floating on a river. When we really feel in sync with the sunrise and sunset, with what God is doing in nature and creation, we disconnect from the trivial pursuits of materialism and the stresses of life that seem so important but in truth matter very little. But sometimes we lose sight of God's beauty in creation because we have tarnished the beauty we were intended to live in.

As we think about what the Promised Land looks like, Paul's teaching about Christ in Colossians is informative:

> He is the *exact* image of the invisible God, the firstborn of creation, *the eternal*. It was by Him that everything was created: the heavens, the earth, all things within and upon them, all things seen and unseen, thrones and dominions, *spiritual* powers and authorities. Every detail was crafted through His design, *by His own hands*, and for His purposes. He has always been! *It is His hand* that holds everything together. He is the head of this body, the church. He is the beginning, the first of those to be reborn from the dead, so that *in every aspect, at every view*, in everything—He is first. God was pleased that all His fullness should *forever* dwell in the Son, who, *as predetermined by God*, bled peace into the world by His death on the cross as God's means of reconciling to Himself the whole creation—all things in heaven and all things on earth.[43]

If God created all things and is reconciling all things, surely we have entered into a sacred trust to care for His remarkable work. If we are to live in a land of promise, we will have to make decisions that help us return our infected land to its original abundance. Harris County, where I live, is in constant competition with Los Angeles for the title "Filthiest Air in the United States." How many kids do you remember having asthma when you were growing up? I don't think I knew of any until I was in college. A public school teacher in my church recently informed me that 90 percent of her inner city class has asthma. According to a program of the Texas Department of State Health Services,

> In Texas in 2007, there were an estimated 876,000 (13.6%) children (0–17 years of age) with reported lifetime asthma and 586,000 (9.1%) children with reported current asthma. . . . The asthma hospitalization rate for all ages in Texas was 10.9 per 10,000 residents, accounting for more than 25,000 hospitalizations and $446.8 million in total hospital charges. From 1999 to 2005, there were a total of 1,831 deaths in Texas due to asthma with a mortality rate of 1.39 per 100,000.[44]

Children die on a regular basis because they can't breathe the air. This is not just a government problem (although I hope the government can help clean up the air); as people of faith we must decide how God wants us to care for the earth.

But a caution is warranted here. There is a whole movement of environmentalism that feels a little bit like the legalism I grew up with around a different set of moral issues. In that setting you could tell if someone was *really* a Christian because they drank soda instead of wine. We could easily switch out this scenario for those who use or don't use environmentally safe lightbulbs, or have waterless urinals, or use biodegradable cups. I'm not interested in life changes that come as a result of guilt or intimidation. I don't think that kind of change is sustainable. But I am interested in sustainable changes that make the air our children breathe less toxic.

We recently exchanged the last few lightbulbs in our household with the new fluorescent incandescent bulbs. As we evaluated what that switch is worth, I found this on the Energy Star website:

> If every household in the US would change the five lightbulbs that they use most often, the country could take 21 coal-fired power plants off line tomorrow. That would keep 1 trillion pounds of poisonous gasses and soot out of the air we breathe. It would be the equivalent of taking 8 million cars off the road.

As you pray the following prayer with me, contemplate what, if any, changes you need to make. As we begin again to connect with creation, I hope you can take some time today to be outside. We desperately need to connect with God in His creation. Just sit in it. Soak in all of God's beauty and begin to ask what it is you can do to care for God's creation.

Prayer

Dear God, we come to You seeking inspiration and direction. Instead of trying to make up new rules and regulations, God, we want You to birth within us Your vision of the Promised Land, Your expression of love and creation. Give us the heart and energy to care for and preserve Your creation. As we think about what this Promised Land looks like, we imagine a place where children are healthy and well, where people work the lands and waters with reverence, and where people give as much or more than they take. God, just as You moved two million people in the Exodus, take us into Your vision of a reconciled world. Let us always be about Your business. Amen.

DEZI IN UGANDA

Dezi lives with his aunt and four other children in western Uganda. Subsistence farming is how the people in his village make a living, and Dezi's aunt sometimes finds work helping other farmers. They grow beans, bananas, and cassava, working the stony soil to survive. Dezi likes singing and running with his friends, and helps out at home by carrying water and gardening. Pray that in Dezi's community, clean water will become available so that children no longer have to deal with stomach illnesses and parasites. Pray that Dezi will know Jesus and grow up to be a bold leader who helps people live at peace and have their needs met.

Day 31

Today and tomorrow we will meditate on the sermon given by Stephen in Acts 7. It has much to tell us about our own journey to the Promised Land. Stephen summarizes the story of God's people in a dramatic and instructive way. As we prepare to read and reflect on this sermon, please pray with me that the abundance of the land of promise will be revealed in our lives today.

God, we believe that You are taking us to a place where there will be abundance for all. Give us the insight, wisdom, creativity, and resources to rid the world of the great divide between those who have and those who have not. We realize that the resources You have given us are a blessing, not a curse, and we need to learn to utilize them well. May we see extreme poverty end in our lifetime. May we give from the overflow of our hearts. May we know in our own lives how much is too much—and seek wisdom in how to share. May we come to You asking how we can care for one another well, and how we can provide for those in dire need. May God give each of us the wisdom to walk the path of generosity. Lead us, Lord, to the Promised Land, where everyone has enough.

I believe Stephen's sermon is one of the greatest ever preached. Although he knows what's coming for him—people with rocks—and he knows this is the last sermon he will ever preach, he breaks into one of the most beautiful summaries of God's narrative I have ever heard. Hear Stephen's final words:

High Priest: *What do you have to say for yourself?* Are these accusations accurate?

Stephen: Brothers, fathers, please listen to me. Our glorious God revealed Himself to our common ancestor Abraham, when he lived far away in Mesopotamia before he immigrated to Haran. God gave him this command: "Leave your country. Leave your family *and your inheritance.* Move into unknown territory, where I will show you a new homeland." First, he left Chaldea *in southern Mesopotamia* and settled in Haran until his father died. Then God led him still farther from his original home—until he settled here, in our land. *But at that point,* God still hadn't given him any of this land as his permanent possession—not even the footprint under his sandal actually belonged to him yet. But God did give Abraham a promise—a promise that yes, someday, the entire land would indeed belong to him and his descendants. *Of course, this promise was all the more amazing because* at that moment, Abraham had no descendants at all.

God said that Abraham's descendants would first live in a foreign country as resident aliens, *as refugees,* for 400 years. During this time, they would be enslaved and treated horribly. *But that would not be the end of the story.* God promised, "I will judge the nation that enslaves them," and "I will bring them to this mountain to serve Me." God gave him the covenant ritual of circumcision *as a sign of His sacred promise.* When Abraham fathered his son, Isaac, he performed this ritual of circumcision on the eighth day. Then Isaac fathered Jacob, and Jacob fathered the twelve patriarchs.

The patriarchs were jealous of *their brother* Joseph, so they sold him as a slave into Egypt. Even so, God was with him; and *time after time,* God rescued Joseph from whatever trials befell him. God gave Joseph the favor and wisdom *to overcome each adversity* and eventually to win the confidence and respect of *his captors, including* Pharaoh, the king of Egypt himself. So Pharaoh entrusted his whole nation and his whole household to Joseph's stewardship. *Some time later,* a terrible famine spread through the entire region—from Canaan down to Egypt—and everyone suffered greatly. Our ancestors, *living here in the region of Canaan,* could find nothing to eat. Jacob heard that Egypt had stores of grain; so he sent our forefathers, *his sons, to procure food* there. Later, when they returned to Egypt a second time, Joseph revealed his true identity to them. He also told Pharaoh his family story.

Joseph then invited his father Jacob and all his clan to come and live with him in Egypt. So Jacob came, along with 75 extended family members. After their deaths, their remains were brought back to this land so they could be buried in the same tomb where Abraham *had buried Sarah* (he had purchased the tomb for a certain amount of silver from the family of Hamor in *the town of* Shechem).

Still God's promise to Abraham had not yet been fulfilled, but the time for that fulfillment was drawing very near. In the meantime, our ancestors living in Egypt rapidly multiplied. Eventually a new king came to power—one who had not known Joseph *when he was the most powerful man in Egypt.* This new leader *feared the growing population of our ancestors and* manipulated them for his own benefit, eventually seeking to control their population by forcing them to abandon their infants so they would die. Into this horrible situation *our ancestor* Moses was born, and he was a beautiful child in God's eyes. He was raised for three months in his father's home, and then he was abandoned *as the brutal regime required.* However, Pharaoh's daughter found, adopted, and raised him as her own son. So Moses learned the culture and wisdom of the Egyptians and became a powerful man—both as an intellectual and as a leader. When he reached the age of 40, his heart drew him to visit his kinfolk, our ancestors, the Israelites. During his visit, he saw one of our people being wronged, and he took sides with our people by killing an Egyptian. He thought his kinfolk would recognize him as their God-given liberator, but they didn't realize *who he was and what he represented.*

The next day Moses was walking among the Israelites again when he observed a fight—but this time, it was between two Israelites. He intervened and tried to reconcile the men. "You two are brothers," he said. "Why do you attack each other?" But the aggressor pushed Moses away and responded *with contempt*: "Who made you our prince and judge? Are you going to slay me *and hide my body* as you did with the Egyptian yesterday?" Realizing this murder had not gone unnoticed, he quickly escaped Egypt and lived as a refugee in the land of Midian. He *married there and* had two sons.

Forty more years passed. One day while Moses was in the desert near Mount Sinai, a heavenly messenger appeared to him in the flames of a burning bush. The phenomenon intrigued Moses; and as he approached for a closer look, he heard a voice—the voice of the Lord: "I am the God of your own fathers, the God of Abraham, Isaac, and Jacob." This terrified Moses—he began to tremble and looked away in fear. The voice continued: "Take off your sandals *and stand barefoot on the ground in My presence*, for this ground is holy ground. I have avidly watched how My people are being mistreated by the Egyptians. I have heard their groaning *at the treatment of their oppressors.* I am descending *personally* to rescue them. So get up. I'm sending you to Egypt."

Now remember: this was the same Moses who had been rejected by his kinfolk when they said, "Who made you our prince and judge?" This man, *rejected by his own people,* was the one God had truly sent, commissioned by the heavenly messenger who appeared in the bush, to be their leader and deliverer.[45]

I struggle with impatience. I want what I want when I want it. And the world seems willing to satisfy my taste for having things right away. If I get the urge to read a book, for example, I don't want to wait for it to become available at the library. I don't want to wait for it to arrive in the mail. I don't even want to go to the bookstore. I want it now, and because I'm able to download the book in seconds, I get it now.

At 40 years of age Moses steps forward to free his people. But his people do not see him as a rescuer, so he flees to Midian and waits another 40 years. At this point God's people have been slaves for four hundred years. So when God shows up in a burning bush declaring that He sees the suffering of His people, Moses may have been tempted to reply (as I would have), "What's taken you so long! It took four hundred years to see that we needed some help?!" And then, after four centuries of waiting, the Israelites escape only to wander in the wilderness for another 40 years.

And here I am, learning to wait. Struggling to eat a simple but plentiful diet for 40 days, waiting for revelation, waiting for celebration. I have so much to learn, but I'm grateful God continues to teach me. He is still active and present in His redemptive work within a culture that is forever seeking immediate gratification. Possibly, He's waiting for us to tune in.

Prayer

God, teach me what it means to wait. May my faith be strengthened as I see the ways that You provide in Your time. Amen.

DOUJNIE IN HAITI

Doujnie's smile is beautiful—so beautiful and full of joy that it is difficult to imagine the hardships she has endured for most of her life. She flashed that smile as clean water flowed from the newly repaired pump in her rural community in Haiti. "We used to walk a very long way for dirty water," she says, "which made my children sick." Like so many women around the world, Doujnie shouldered the burdensome task of collecting water every single day. But no longer. Again, she smiles. "This pump is a very good thing." Please pray for the women and children who walk long distances to collect the water that so often makes them sick.

Day 32

After four centuries of slavery in Egypt, God delivered His people. But He did not fade into the background of history to let them find their own way. At this point He seemed to intervene relentlessly on their behalf. They weren't just left out there to walk over their own footprints for decades.

Many of us can attest to the joy in our hearts when we are in step with God—that resounding heartbeat that seems to want to burst out of our chest with adoration and profound love. But most of us also know the despair felt in the times when we have veered off course and stomped, sweated, trudged, paved, or otherwise connived our own way. The children of Israel were being reminded of the importance of trusting God. His path is the right path—though as we see in Stephen's story, it may not be the easiest path. Read the rest of the last sermon he ever preached.

Stephen: Moses indeed led our ancestors to freedom, and he performed miraculous signs and wonders in Egypt, at the Red Sea, and in the wilderness over a period of 40 years. This Moses promised our ancestors, "The Eternal One your God will raise up from among your people a Prophet who will be like me." This is the same one who led the people to Mount Sinai, where a heavenly messenger spoke to him and our ancestors, and who received the living message of God to give to us.

But our ancestors still resisted. They again pushed Moses away and refused to follow him. In their hearts, they were ready to return to *their former slavery in Egypt. While Moses was on the mountain communing with God,* they begged Aaron to make idols to lead them. "We have no idea what happened to this fellow, Moses, who brought us from Egypt," they said. So they made a calf as their new god, and they even sacrificed to it and celebrated an object they had fabricated *as if it were their God.*

And you remember what God did next: He let them go. He turned from them and let them follow their idolatrous path—worshiping sun, moon, and stars *just as their unenlightened neighbors did.* The prophet *Amos* spoke for God *about this horrible betrayal*:

> Did you offer Me sacrifices or give Me offerings
> during your 40-year wilderness journey, you Israelites?
> *No, but* you have taken along your sacred tent for the wor-
> ship of Moloch,
> and you honored the star of Rompha, your false god.
> So, if you want to worship your man-made images,
> you may do so—beyond Babylon.

Now recall that our ancestors had a sacred tent in the wilderness, the tent God directed Moses to build according to the pattern revealed to him. When Joshua led our ancestors to dispossess the nations God drove out before them, our ancestors carried this sacred tent. It remained here in the land until the time of David. David found favor with God and asked Him for permission to build a permanent structure *(rather than a portable tent)* to honor Him. It was, of course, Solomon who actually built God's house. Yet we all know the Most High God doesn't actually dwell in structures made by human hands, as the prophet *Isaiah* said,

> "Since My throne is heaven
> and since My footstool is earth—
> What kind of structure can you build to contain Me?
> What *man-made* space could provide Me a resting place?"
> asks the Eternal One.
> "Didn't I make all things with My own hand?"

You stubborn, stiff-necked people! Sure, you are physically Jews, but you are no different from outsiders in your hearts and ears! You are just like your ancestors, constantly fighting against the Holy Spirit. Didn't your ancestors persecute the prophets? First, they killed those prophets who predicted the coming of the Just One, and now you have betrayed and murdered the Just One Himself! Yes, you received the law as given by heavenly messengers, but you haven't kept the law which you received.

Upon hearing this, *his audience could contain themselves no longer.* They boiled in fury at Stephen; they clenched their jaws and ground their teeth. But Stephen was filled with the Holy Spirit. Gazing upward into heaven, he saw *something they couldn't see:* the glory of God, and Jesus standing at His right hand.

Stephen: Look, I see the heavens opening! I see the Son of man standing at the right hand of God!

At this, they covered their ears and started shouting. The whole crowd rushed at Stephen, converged on him, dragged him out of the city, and stoned him.

They laid their coats at the feet of a young man named Saul, while they were pelting Stephen with rocks.

Stephen *(as rocks fell upon him)*: Lord Jesus, receive my spirit.

Then he knelt *in prayer*, shouting at the top of his lungs,

Stephen: Lord, do not hold this evil against them!

Those were his final words; then he fell asleep *in death.*[46]

In the next several days, we are going to look beyond Exodus and Numbers and into the Jesus narrative. We will see the character of God's people when He is allowed to deal with their hearts—we will see these people truly experience a change that allows them to enter into the Promised Land.

We have been in the wilderness too long. Today my prayer is that God would soften our hearts and open our ears. I am confident that when our ears are open to hear God speak, God speaks. When our hearts are soft and able to feel His hand as it guides us, we can follow in obedience, and beautiful things happen. I have seen it time and again—the Holy Spirit is truly active in teaching us all. But what will we do if our calling leads us into greater challenges? Will we have faith as Stephen did to speak and live the truth even while those around us are gathering stones?

Prayer

God, do Your work within us. Give us the wisdom to know how to share ourselves, our lives, and our resources with one another as well as those scattered abroad. God, we don't want to give out of legalism, obligation, or guilt. We pray that You will show us how to give. Everything we have is from You. Although Your children spent 40 years (an awfully long time to us) in rebellion and angst and idolatry, they came to a place where they began to trust You. They dealt with their complaining spirits, and You allowed them into this place of abundance. Christ is our passageway through the great sea. Christ is our manna from heaven. Christ is our water in dry places. We want to see You fully, Lord Jesus, just as Stephen could see You as the stones fell upon him. We ask that our focus would remain on You. That our worship would truly change us. Your love is unyielding. Amen.

MISHA IN GUATEMALA

Misha knew that many children in her village in Guatemala were sick because the water they drank and bathed in came from a nearby river, but that wasn't the whole story. "The kids walk around with no shoes," she explains. "They put things in their mouths and don't wash their hands.  We see them put their fingers in their noses, and we did not realize that it is bad for them." When a Living Water mission team traveled to her village to drill a new well for the community, they also taught health and hygiene lessons about things like hand washing, germ transmission, brushing teeth, and keeping their new pump clean. "The hygiene lessons were good," Misha said, "because many times, we knew that we should be doing something, but we did not know what to do. Now, we know." Pray for the eradication of water-borne illnesses through the establishment of water wells, sanitation, and hygiene education.

Day 33

Have you ever looked at a digitally recreated map of the journey Moses and God's children took through the wilderness? It is depressing. For 40 years they wandered around in circles. It would be funny if it did not hit so close to home. I have also spent 40 years of my life making some of the same mistakes. Just when I think I am ready for the Promised Land I fall back into old patterns and have to take another lap around the wilderness. Thankfully, in other areas of my life I have experienced real victory. How do we know when our ache and struggle is purposeful (leading to redemption) or destructive (headed back to the same mistakes repeated over and over again)? Surely the children of Israel believed many times they were ready for God to lead them to victory. How do we know that our time has come? To find the answers to these questions we have to examine our sin and restlessness carefully.

I do not exhibit traits of obsessive-compulsive disorder, but when it comes to public restrooms, I am quite particular. When my kids were younger, the reality of how much I despise public restrooms came to light because kids, especially when they are really little, don't understand the difference between a toilet and a couch. My little ones would have hugged the urinal if I let them. When I began taking my kids into public restrooms, I realized this was one of those situations where I was going to teach them my own rules of conduct: "When we go into the men's room, don't touch anything. Flush with your foot. Wash your hands. Use soap! And use the paper towel to get you through the door unharmed." I take this very seriously.

It has occurred to me that most Christians view their experiences in this world like I view a trip to the public restroom. How can we get in and get out and not get our hands dirty? We become so afraid that "those" people will infect us with their sin problem. So instead of connecting with others, we evangelize by dropping tracts on tables or preaching at people rather than getting to know them. We hope the gospel will invade their lives without us having to actually be present. But true Christianity is all about presence (the incarnation). We forget we are equally tainted by sin: wronging God and one another and defeating ourselves. None of us is better than the next. We do not need to live in fear that we will fall out of grace or be lured into sin by embracing broken people on their journey. Many times, sin (when you see it up close in the lives of people) is actually not very attractive.

Sometimes sin seems most attractive when we are steeped in the rules of a religious culture. Remember the movie *Footloose*? In that legalistic town every forbidden thing looked attractive to a group of young people who were not allowed to dance and enjoy themselves. Rules have a way of making us long to break them. But when I hang out with a substance abuser, I don't watch him or her and think, "This is exactly what I am going to do tomorrow night. This is a great way to live life." Listen as Paul delves into the mysteries of law and sin.

My brothers and sisters, in the same way, you have died when it comes to the law because of *your connection with* the body of the Anointed One. His death—*and your death with Him*—frees you to belong to the One who was raised from the dead so we can bear fruit for God. As we were living in the flesh, the law *could not solve the problem of sin; it* only awakened our lust for more and cultivated the fruit of death in our bodily members. But now that we have died to those chains that imprisoned us, we have been released from the law to serve in a new Spirit-empowered life, not the old written code.

So what is the story? Is the law itself sin? Absolutely not! *It is the exact opposite.* I would never have known what sin is if it were not for the law. *For example,* I would not have known that desiring something that belongs to my neighbor is sin if the law had not said, "You are not to covet." Sin took advantage of the commandment to create a constant stream of greed and desire within me; *I began to want everything.* You see, apart from the law, sin lies dormant. There was a time when I was living without the law, but the commandment came *and changed everything*: sin came to life, and I died. This commandment was supposed to bring life; but in my experience, it brought death. Sin took advantage of the commandment, tricked me, and exploited it in order to kill me. So *hear me out:* the law is holy and its commandments are holy, right, and good.

So did the good *law* bring about my death? Absolutely not! It was sin that killed me, *not the law.* It's the nature of sin to produce death through what is good and exploit the commandments to multiply sin's vile effects. This is what we know: the law comes from the spiritual realm. *My problem is that* I am of the fallen human realm, owned by sin, *which tries to keep me in its service.*[47]

Paul is clear about the fact that rules do not have the power to rescue us; in fact, they seem to bring out the worst in us by exposing our sin. Our struggle with food has served the same purpose. It has exposed our restlessness and offered us the chance to find deeper joy in the arms of our Savior. The problem of sin comes from the inside, not the outside. And when we begin to trust in God more fully, we will be changed. Our ongoing transformation will lead us to a land of promise rather than another tour through familiar wilderness terrain.

Prayer

Thank You, God, that You can use all things for Your good. Thank You for allowing us to identify with those who wrestle with the law, with those who struggle to remain clean and pure and cannot help but fail. Thank You for the person who reaches out to me when I am heading the wrong way, when I have been defeated by this world or my own thoughts. I need Your guidance, Your rest, Your strength. I know today without a doubt that I need Your grace.

May I take these gifts into the places You send me, that these too would be used for Your greater good. Amen.

JOCELYN IN ECUADOR

Jocelyn lives with her parents and siblings in southern Ecuador. Malaria and typhoid fever are common in this tropical area, where some people work on banana plantations but unemployment is high. Many people eat only once a day, and malnutrition makes it hard to recover from basic illnesses. The city has a poor trash collection system, so garbage is either burned or left to rot in the streets and ditches. Jocelyn helps at home by caring for the other children, making beds, and helping in the kitchen. She is an average student and likes singing and playing basketball at the church where she receives support through Compassion. Pray that God will keep her family healthy, and that Jocelyn will understand how deeply Jesus loves her.

Day 34

There are only a few things on this planet that I truly hate. It is a very short list that includes the Chicago Cubs, squeaking Styrofoam, religious arrogance, and cancer. I have felt the pain of this evil disease and lost too many people that I love to this predatory infection. It robs families of loved ones long before their time.

I pray often for cures and more effective treatments. But as much as I despise cancer and see it as a thief, I have also come to recognize a hidden blessing that it brings in its fatal hands—a unique chance to die well. How do you think you might respond to this opportunity? I'll never forget the unexpected flood of emotions I felt when I sat down to watch *My Life,* a movie starring Michael Keaton. In the film he learns he is terminally ill and will likely die before his wife (played by Nicole Kidman) gives birth to their first child. With a video camera in hand he sets off on a journey to pass on his story to his unborn child and along the way finds redemption, restoration, and reconciliation. The death we fear has the opportunity to bring with it a new perspective on life.

The truth is we are all going to die, so why not go ahead and live like we are dying? We often live as though we are invincible. We try to fool ourselves with new, progressive anti-aging technologies and surgeries, making death seem like a distant dream, yet our days here on earth are numbered. Those who die at peace about eternity, reconciled to those they love, and having no regrets about what is left unsaid experience a rare blessing. Listen to some of the words Moses sang to the people of Israel moments before he ascended the mountain to make his hospice with God:

Moses: The Eternal will judge His people
and have mercy on His servants

When He sees they have no strength left
    and they're all gone, both slave and free.
Then He'll say *about Israel,* "Now where are their gods,
    the rocks where they took shelter,
The gods who ate the fat of their sacrifices
    and drank the wine they offered?
Let them get up and help you, *Israel*!
    Let them protect you!"

Eternal One: Now do you see that I am the One
    and there is no other God besides Me?
I have power over life and death;
    I wound, and I heal;
       no one can resist My power!
I'm lifting up My hand toward the sky *to take an oath,*
    and I swear, "As I live forever,
When I sharpen My flashing sword
    and use it to bring about justice,
I'll give My enemies what they deserve
    and pay back those who hate Me!
I'll get My arrows drunk with blood,
    the blood of the dead and the prisoners,
And My sword will feast on flesh,
    on the heads with their uncut hair of the enemy leaders!"

Moses: You nations, celebrate with His *covenant* people
    because He's going to avenge the blood of His servants.
He'll give His enemies what they deserve
    and atone for His land and His people.[48]

Prayer

God, *we ask as people of faith that You would teach us what it means to truly set our eyes on heaven and live as those who do not fear death. Prompt us toward forgiveness, restoration, and reconciliation so that we might see every day we have on this earth as a gift from You. We thank You that this life is not what we live for, but it is our unique chance to be about Your work and tell Your story to so many who need to hear it. Lead us into conversations about life and death and give us words of hope so that hope might replace fear. Amen.*

CHIEF VARNEY IN LIBERIA

"This is where we would get our drinking water," Chief Varney said, indicating a muddy swamp. "We had been suffering a very long time, for safe drinking water to come here." Varney is the chief elder of Gbenneh Hill Town, a village of 150 people in western Liberia. During the long dry season, when the water hole dried up, villagers—including children—had to walk more than ten miles for water. Determined to find an alternative before the next dry season began, Chief Varney organized the men of the village to dig a well by hand, but the diggers met a layer of rock at about twenty feet and were forced to give up. Around the same time Living Water came to Gbenneh Hill and drilled a brand-new well in the center of the village. "Since using this water, we have not experienced sickness like diarrhea and cholera," Chief Varney reported. "Thank God for providing safe drinking water for us in this community." Pray for village leaders who are determined to create better conditions for their people.

FEAST DAY: Jesus Enters the City

As we embark on the final week of our fasting journey, let us walk as fellow pilgrims with Jesus as He enters Jerusalem. The last 34 days have not been perfect; like the children of Israel we have stumbled many times along the way. But we have been sustained despite our failures, and we now walk into the Holy City with our Savior. Everyone expected King Jesus to enter in great power on a prodigious stallion, but startlingly He entered on a baby donkey. He was more than what He seemed.

As we contemplate this triumphal entry of our King, we have stumbled upon the great paradox of our faith: God, the source of all power in the universe, embraced weakness to bring triumph. Yet we who seek to follow the path of Jesus often mistakenly chase after power, might, and strength as the symbols of God's presence with us.

Have you come to your wit's end a few times during this fast? I hope so. Have you failed to keep your fast at any point by either mere forgetfulness, willful rebellion, or utter apathy? I have. The last 34 days are not a testament to our power, strength of character, or self-control. Remember: it is the journey to surrender our struggles, to gain insight into our cravings, and renewed reliance on God that is transforming.

The fact that Jesus rode this baby donkey through the cheering crowds made a statement to everyone who saw Him: Jesus did not come to fight, He came to surrender. As we march toward the city, like Jesus, we too are surrendering. The image of Jesus on this tiny beast communicates more truth than words can contain, but it was the scent that Jesus carried with Him that the crowds were not likely to forget. Do you remember the aroma Jesus carried with Him?

Six days before the Passover feast, Jesus journeyed to the village of Bethany, to the home of Lazarus who had recently been raised from the dead, where they hosted Him for dinner. Martha was busy serving *as the hostess*, Lazarus reclined at the table with Him, and Mary took a pound of fine ointment, pure nard (which is *both rare and* expensive), and anointed Jesus' feet with it, and then wiped them with her hair. As the pleasant fragrance of this extravagant ointment filled the entire house, Judas Iscariot, one of His disciples (who was plotting to betray Jesus), began to speak.

Judas Iscariot: *How could she pour out* this vast amount of fine oil? Why didn't she sell it? It is worth nearly a year's wages; the money could have been given to the poor.

This had nothing to do with Judas's desire to help the poor. The truth is he served as the treasurer, and he helped himself to the money from the common pot at every opportunity.

Jesus: Leave her alone. She has observed this custom in anticipation of the day of My burial. The poor are ever present, but I will be leaving.

Word spread of Jesus' presence, and a large crowd was gathering to see Jesus and the formerly deceased Lazarus, whom He had brought back from the dead. The chief priests were secretly plotting Lazarus's murder since, because of him, many Jews were leaving their teachings and believing in Jesus.

The next day, a great crowd of people who had come to the festival heard that Jesus was coming to Jerusalem, so they gathered branches of palm trees to wave as they celebrated His arrival.[49]

Take a minute. Imagine the air filled with rare oil pressed from flowering plants found in the Himalayas. An entire jar of nard, a very thick essential oil valued at one year's wages (in today's

193

dollars, about $45,000) poured out all at once. The aroma of this extravagant gift carried through the crowd just as the story of Jesus spread among all peoples. Certain scents from my past will stay with me for a lifetime: the smell of my grandmother's kitchen, my first trip to the ocean, the fragrance of my newborn children. The unmistakable scent of nard must have reminded each of these people of this event for the rest of their lives. "He looked like any one of us, downing the hill on a colt . . . but the air about Him was sweet and rich."

As we face our own problems, as the enemy seeks to destroy us, how might we learn from the Teacher? His defense—utter vulnerability—allowed Him to choose a path of redemption. Do we really believe in something bigger than ourselves? Are we ready to follow Jesus's direction?

Prayer

By Martin Tuinzing

At church today I wrote this on my iPad during worship. As Chris began to speak about Jesus, I temporarily lost the battle to dam the flood of frustration and loneliness and pain and longing for love. I literally cried out, choking back tears (some, anyway) and wept as quietly as I could (but quite loud), surrounded by fellow worshippers. How I longed for the words spoken by Chris to transpire, that Jesus would save me, save me there today! How my need for Him won the day in my sorrow and these were the words spilled . . .

> He sees me when I can't
> This trickle beyond my strength
> It hurts too much to sing
> Attached to the very deep
> The essence of me
> The grazed waters of my soul
> My whole being is moved
> The whole basin is stirred

194

This tear just won't stop running
Split down the middle, I choke I weep.
Oh my fear, His love, so steep . . .
I sit in His assembly
How this grief wracks my chest
How I hope, I cry, I look up
To be seen, to be heard, to be loved.

ZARIA IN SIERRA LEONE

Zaria used to sleep among the rocks during the dry season, waiting for a trickle of cloudy water to signal that the spring had recharged. During the rainy season, things weren't much better, because the torrents of water picked up every bit of trash and effluent in the river's path. Today, Zaria and her neighbors in Sierra Leone don't have to sleep among the rocks. They don't have to drink water with trash in it. They enjoy clean, safe water from repaired water points around their village. Pray for people who still wait for water to come.

Day 35

As we walk this 40-day path, we are walking in solidarity with Jesus, one another, and those whom Jesus loves—namely, the poor. Along the way we find ourselves learning how remarkable our Messiah truly is. As we examine His teachings, His life, and His love, we find a new sense of inspiration each day.

In no place is Jesus more remarkable than in His relationships. Most of us can remember when we began to feel pressure to associate ourselves with the "in" crowd, to be around those with power, prestige, and popularity. Jesus sought the exact opposite. He was drawn to the outcast, the hungry, the tax collectors, the lepers, the women, and the children—who in that culture had no power and were often looked down upon. In fact, He often offended the powerful; His life was an indictment of their values. When the disciples of John the Baptist came to Him (as many had) asking, "Explain to us more fully, we need to know if you are the Messiah, the one we have been waiting on," Jesus responded as follows:

Jesus (to John's disciples): Go and tell John what you've witnessed with your own eyes and ears: the blind are seeing again, the lame are walking again, the lepers are clean again, the deaf hear again, the dead live again, and good news is preached to the poor. Whoever is not offended by Me is blessed indeed.[50]

Jesus cites His love for the poor and outcast as evidence of His messianic identity, and He calls us to the same love.

In John 15:9–15 we hear Jesus speak to a group of disciples who are afraid He is going to leave and abandon them. They are doubtful and unsure about their future mission. In just a few words Jesus assures them powerfully.

Jesus: I have loved you as the Father has loved Me. Abide in My love. Follow My example in obeying the Father's commandments and receiving His love. If you obey My commandments, you will stay in My love. I want you to know the delight I experience, to find ultimate satisfaction, which is why I am telling you all of this.

My commandment to you is this: love others as I have loved you. There is no greater way to love than to give your life for your friends. You celebrate our friendship if you obey this command. I don't call you servants any longer; servants don't know what the master is doing, but I have told you everything the Father has said to Me. I call you friends.

I have read the Gospel of John many times, but I never fail to get goose bumps when I hear Jesus refer to us as friends. At times it can feel like the force behind everything, the animating power of the universe, is an immoveable, unbiased energy that simply does what it does without thinking at all of our existence. The above passage teaches us how untrue this view is. The power behind the universe has a name—Jesus—and He is our friend.

We all have felt alone at one time or another; each of us has experienced the darkness and depression of isolation. During these times it is a great comfort to know Jesus has declared Himself our friend. Jesus always listens, always cares, and is always willing to reach into the depths of our deepest problems and lead us to a new and better day. Just as Jesus's friendship is a great comfort to us, we are to be friends with those whom Jesus cares about, the poor.

If Jesus is our ultimate friend and He calls us into loving friendship and community, and if we will be identified by our love for others, how will we carry this 40-day journey of solidarity with the poor into the rest of our lives? How will we reorient our journey, our friendships, our expectations? Will we befriend those whom Jesus would befriend? Care for those whom Jesus would care for? If so, we will experience the profound ways Jesus's love changes the world.

Prayer

Lord, Your life changed the world—there is no problem that grace doesn't solve. Thank You that grace is enough. As we interact with You through the Scriptures and prayer, help us to become more graceful with others, to see with new eyes, to let go of things that separate us from those You love. We need this in our lives, Lord. We need to spill out grace so that we can receive the blessing of Your freedom. As we start to emerge from this journey, give us the blessing of taking another's hand. Amen.

KAHKASHAN AND BAASIM IN INDIA

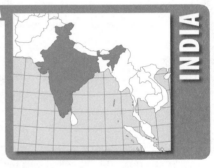

A cluster of homes perches on a rocky hill near the edge of a national forest in the south Indian state of Kerala. For many years the nearest source of water was at the end of a treacherous half-mile journey into the valley; when it rained, the slippery downhill path was nearly impassable. Kahkashan and her husband, Baasim, were afraid to walk to the well, especially during the rainy season. "We were stuck," Kahkashan says. "We didn't know what to do." A local pastor put Kahkashan in touch with Living Water International's south India team. When the team arrived, the whole community turned out to help—Hindu, Muslim, and Christian alike. "When they came," Kahkashan said, "we were all so happy—everyone worked together." Today, a village that once had nothing in common shares not only a water well but the experience of working together to help it become a reality. "We can talk to our neighbors about Jesus now . . . about why we follow him," Kahkashan said. Baasim, standing nearby with their son, nodded and put his hand on the boy's head. "And this one will grow up without getting sick." Please pray for the spirit of true community to pervade villages like this one through the gift of clean water in Jesus's name.

Day 36

When we contemplate the life and teachings of Jesus, we often make certain mistakes. We fail to consider the historical context of Jesus's words or we take those words out of the context of the larger story of Scripture. We emphasize one truth in a way that dismisses the complete truth. The best example of this is our emphasis on the divinity of Christ to the detriment of our understanding of His humanity. It is a beautiful thing to accept the reality that God drew near to humanity by coming to earth, but that is not the Christian story. What makes the story astonishing is that God came in the form of 100 percent humanity. Jesus did not have a different kind of anatomy from any other man. He endured the discomforts of puberty, felt the ache of tired muscles, experienced injuries and falls, and knew very well the misery of sickness.

When we read passages in which Jesus speaks out of this humanity, we often ignore or skip past them. But I believe these passages most fully explain the radical love of God, which we desperately need to experience. In the following, Philip and Andrew appeal for Jesus to address Greek pilgrims who long to meet Him. Jesus responds by explaining more fully what will happen in the days that follow:

Jesus: *(to Philip and Andrew)*: The time has come for the Son of Man to be glorified. I tell you the truth: unless a grain of wheat is planted in the ground and dies, it remains a solitary seed. But when it is planted, it produces in death a great harvest. The one who loves this life will lose it, and the one who despises it in this world will have life forevermore. Anyone who serves Me must follow My path; anyone who serves Me will want to be where I am, and he will be honored by the Father. My spirit is low and unsettled. How can I ask the Father to save Me from this hour? This hour is the purpose for which I have come *into the world. But what I can say is this:* "Father, glorify Your name!"

Suddenly a voice echoed from the heavens.

The Father: I have glorified My name. And again I will bring glory *in this hour that will resound throughout time.*

The crowd of people surrounding Jesus were confused.

Some in the Crowd: It sounded like thunder.

Others: A heavenly messenger spoke to Him.

Jesus: The voice you hear has not spoken for My benefit, but for yours. Now judgment comes upon this world, *and everything will change.* The tyrant of this world, *Satan,* will be thrown out. When I am lifted up from the earth, then all of humanity will be drawn to Me.

These words foreshadowed the nature of His death.[51]

Does it disturb you to hear Jesus acknowledge a sense of dread about the brutal death that lies before Him? Does it seem un-Christlike that He is "low and unsettled"? We want Jesus to be settled about all things, but no human being joyfully anticipates suffering. It is instinctive to flinch. Jesus is not deterred, and He is in no way contemplating disobedience when it comes to the Father's plan for Him. Obedience does not imply a syrupy sweet disposition at all times; in fact, syrupy sweetness would seem inappropriate for one facing a brutal execution.

Too often our understanding of Jesus is distorted. We think of Him as a divine robot on a sacred mission; He was not. Jesus felt human emotions, and so do we. Ignoring our own feelings of being low and unsettled does not help us walk the path of obedience. We must learn to acknowledge our fears, doubts, and disappointments, and learn what it means to be obedient even when we don't feel like it. Do you have any feelings that you are trying to hide or mask? Will you take the time to acknowledge them to God today and pray for obedient faith?

Prayer

Father, we are truly thankful for the life of Jesus, our brother and King. In every way He came to show us how to live—how to celebrate, how to obey, how to lean into You, how to raise the spirits of others, and how to lay our life down to glorify You. His heart was deeply rooted in You, and the rewards of His faithful obedience have covered all past and future generations. Take us to the root too. Bring us to the source of what is so hard to face. Help us accept our own humanity, our own faults and fears. Help us face what we want to avoid. Help us be honest with ourselves and others. Help us not to hide from the truth, and help us keep moving forward even though it may hurt. Show us what we are to take on, be with us as we move through obstacles, pitfalls, and triumphant finishes. May our lives celebrate and honor You to our greatest ability. Amen.

MATEO IN EL SALVADOR

Mateo spent his early childhood running from war. His father joined the country's revolution, so it was up to his mom to keep him safe. Like many Salvadorans, his family frequently moved around to seek refuge. Deep down, Mateo knew there was a better way to live. When Mateo became a Christian, the kingdom of God became the only revolution he wanted to be a part of. As a high school student he started a ministry, playing soccer with prison inmates as a way to build relationships to lead them to Jesus. Today, Mateo is a seminary graduate and a missionary—and helps to lead Living Water's efforts in El Salvador. But Mateo also lives and works in a country with one of the highest murder rates in the Western Hemisphere. Street gangs plague his country's streets and poverty pervades its fields. Please pray that God will protect his spirit, and that he will continue to reflect God's light as he provides clean water in Jesus's name.

Day 37

It has been an eye-opening experience each day to sit down to a meal and (whether I wanted to or not) contemplate the Compassion International children we are connected to who are living in poverty. In the busyness of my world, I typically do not think of them or pray for them enough. Yet they are my friends. On this journey, food has brought us together, and I often have chosen to set an extra place at the table to remind me of their presence. Sometimes we as a family place a photo of one of our sponsor children on our table as a physical reminder that these friends, though they are far away, are part of our family.

It was a rare privilege to have the tables turned a bit during a journey I made to Ecuador. I had the incredible blessing to visit one of the children we sponsor through Compassion International. His name is Brandon David Ruiz Proano. Strong name, right? He is a strong kid at only six years old.

I was able to spoil Brandon with gifts: toys, candies, chocolates (boy, does that kid love chocolate!), art supplies, and a soccer ball. We played together with the art supplies, finger rockets, a dry erase board, and we kicked his new soccer ball around until the lunch bell rang. When it was time to eat, his face lit up. This was clearly the time of day many of the kids had been waiting for. Brandon and I made our way to the small cafeteria area at his church, where his Compassion project is located. We sat together as they brought us a small plate of chicken, rice, and a salad of mixed vegetables. We ate together—this time not around my table, but his. It was one of the most beautiful experiences of my life. It made sense of this journey for me in so many ways. The food had never tasted so good because I shared, for at least a few moments, the joy that Brandon feels when eating a good meal at his Compassion project.

In the presence of Brandon, the words of Jesus in John 14:12–14 finally seemed to make sense:

Jesus: I tell you the truth: whoever believes in Me will be able to do what I have done, but they will do even greater things, because I will return to be with the Father. Whatever you ask for in My name, I will do it so that the Father will get glory from the Son. *Let Me say it again:* if you ask for anything in My name, I will do it.

I always wondered how our works could ever compare to feeding the multitudes or turning water into wine, but as I sat with Brandon I could see the miraculous power of love and generosity. When we pool together our resources, those resources cross entire oceans and become bread from heaven to those on other continents. If you sponsor a child or help to fund a water well, you are part of a miracle.

Prayer

Father, Your love and provision are far reaching. Your miracles never cease. You could drop bread from the sky for Your beloved, and yet You give us the blessing of giving and connecting in Your precious name. May Your Spirit continue to free our hearts and inspire us, Father, to further Your movement of grace and love and equality next door and around the entire world. Amen.

SHORT-TERM MISSION TEAMS

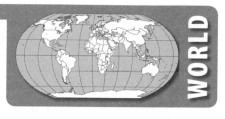

In 2010, Living Water International sent more than a thousand volunteers into the field to see the water crisis firsthand, and to love and serve the world's thirsty. Something amazing always happens on these trips, and it isn't just the water: the American teams go to give to the people who need clean water, but they return having received something even more precious than that. They have encountered Jesus in the thirsty—they have seen Him in their eyes, in the determination of the women to provide better lives for their children, in the smiles and laughter around the new wells, in the joy and generosity of the very people they go to serve. The gospel is good news to be shared, and sharing always works two ways. Please pray for Living Water's short-term mission teams, and for all who advocate on behalf of the world's thirsty, as they encounter Christ among those whom they seek to serve. Pray that these encounters will transform lives, communities, and the world.

Day 38

Ancient kings took power either by peaceful transition after the death of a monarch parent or by building a revolutionary force and seizing power at the right time. All indicators pointed to the latter in the case of King Jesus. He was building a vast following as the crescendo to His tour of miraculous signs and prophetic teachings. His uprising seemed imminent as He approached Jerusalem. But as the crowds gathered, they found Him atop a baby donkey. He entered the Holy City in humility, not grandeur. Can you imagine how many more thousands of people might have taken to the streets if He came bearing a sword? The people were ready to revolt against their Roman oppressors. But Jesus had a different plan, and the disciples who had once fought about who would sit at His right hand when they came to power were confused.

If one is to become king, he must present himself as stately, and Jesus was failing at this. When His cohorts gathered for the Passover feast, they no doubt had every intention of turning this crippled campaign around. It was time for a celebration befitting a king. In the midst of their expectation, Jesus did the unthinkable:

Before the Passover festival began, Jesus was keenly aware that His hour had come to depart from this world and to return to the Father. From beginning to end, Jesus' days were marked by His love for His people. Before Jesus and His disciples gathered for dinner, the adversary filled Judas Iscariot's heart with plans of deceit and betrayal. Jesus, knowing that He had come from God and was going away to God, stood up from dinner and removed His outer garments. He then wrapped Himself in a towel, poured water in a basin, and began to wash the feet of the disciples, drying them with His towel.

Simon Peter *(as Jesus approaches)*: Lord, are You going to wash my feet?

Jesus: Peter, you don't realize what I am doing, but you will understand later.

Peter: You will not wash my feet, now or ever!

Jesus: If I don't wash you, you will have nothing to do with Me.

Peter: Then wash me but don't stop with my feet. Cleanse my hands and head as well.

Jesus: Listen, anyone who has bathed is clean all over except for the feet. But I tell you this, not all of you are clean.

He knew the one with plans of betraying Him, which is why He said, "not all of you are clean." After washing their feet and picking up His garments, He reclined at the table again.

Jesus: Do you understand what I have done to you? You call Me Teacher and Lord, and truly, that is who I am. So if your Lord and Teacher washes your feet, then you should wash one another's feet. I am your example; keep doing what I do. I tell you the truth: a servant is not greater than the master. Those who are sent are not greater than the One who sends them. If you know these things, and if you put them into practice, you will find happiness.[52]

After months of the disciples fighting over who would sit in the seat of power, Jesus turned the tables; the real fight was over the largest foot-washing basin. This was a game changer. It exposed everyone's motives. Suffice it to say, Judas was not pleased. Peter and the others were shell-shocked, but ultimately they did come to understand that service trumps power in the kingdom of God.

Which kingdom are you living in? Have you devoted your life to humble service, or do you avoid it like an infectious disease? Jesus came to change the world, one dirty foot at a time. How about you?

Prayer

God, what is any power on earth compared to You? Yet You became lowly that You might lift us up. With love and determination You turned Your triumphal entry into a death march. As each clopping hoof brought You closer to pain, You didn't miss a step. You stayed in time. But each step You took on this path became greater than the next. Together with Your closest friends, though they couldn't fathom the whole of You, You poured water into a basin and washed the dirt from their traveling feet. The dirt of ages. The dirt of generations. Lord, in an instant You both reveal and heal our hearts. Thank You. You have shown us the map, You have plotted the course, You have made us a place, and You have never deserted us. Lord, may we continue to make our way home. Amen.

ANAYELIS IN COLOMBIA

Anayelis lives in northern Colombia with her mother and grandfather. Her grandfather works part-time and her mother stays at home. In her community, the common diet is rice, fish, and plantains. Job opportunities are scarce, so poor nutrition and regular illness are ongoing problems. Anayelis is an active girl who loves playing games and running around with her friends. Please pray that as she grows, Anayelis will know God's love and that her family will have their needs met.

Day 39

Jesus asked questions of His disciples that exposed their lack of self-awareness. One of these questions came when the disciples were struggling to embrace their true calling. They believed they were called to follow Jesus so they could embrace a position of power. I may not be as outspoken about it, but I often share their sense of entitlement and ambition.

As Jesus was speaking about the things that were to come, Zebedee's wife, whose sons were among Jesus' disciples, came to Jesus with her sons and knelt down before Him to ask a favor.

Jesus: What do you want?

Zebedee's Wife: When the kingdom of God is made manifest, I want one of my boys to sit at Your right hand, and one to sit at Your left hand.

Jesus *(to all three)*: You don't understand what you are asking. Can you drink the cup I am going to drink? Can you be literally washed in baptism just as I have been baptized?

Zebedee Brothers: Of course!

Jesus: Yes, you will drink from My cup, and yes, you will be baptized as I have been. But the thrones to My right and My left are not Mine to grant. My Father has already given those seats to those for whom they were created.

The other ten disciples learned what the Zebedee brothers had asked of Jesus, and they were upset.[53]

"Can you drink the cup I am going to drink?" I was once asked the same question by a tribal chief in rural Liberia. Located on the west coast of Africa, this nation has suffered extreme poverty. I was representing my church on a visit to areas where we would fund new water wells through a movement called the Advent Conspiracy. In most of the communities, we were well received. But when we asked one community if we could see their water source, they seemed particularly angry. They walked us to what you and I would call a swamp, and we asked them about illness and disease. Instead of giving us an answer, the chief of the village turned to me with a blunt command: "Take a drink of this water! Why don't you take a drink of it? Why don't you drink?" He was angry, and I did not know what we had done to offend him. But I could not bear to drink the brown and green water—the only water source this community had.

Soon it became clear that people in this village had been getting very sick from the water. We were there to help, so their anger puzzled me. Why would they be so demonstrably angry to people who were coming to help drill new wells? As we departed I asked a woman in the village this question, and she explained how the chief had recently lost his six-year-old son to cholera from the dirty water, just days before our visit. In some ways, when we asked to see his water source, we were asking him to look upon the weapon that had killed his child. This woman added that many people, including Christians, had promised year after year to help solve their water problem. Year after year the village waited.

When I left, I was determined that our church would help make clean water a reality in their area, and we deployed a team with Living Water International right away. Months later, while I was driving down a Houston highway, a photo came to my phone of that same chief standing next to their new water well. He was brandishing a smile like I had never seen. I long to go back and drink clean water with him.

I don't know what God has been asking you to do on this journey. Are you being called to a new lifestyle, one that is marked more by generosity than consumption? I doubt that Jesus is calling you to

210

seek power, prestige, and popularity. But when He gives you those things, you have a remarkable chance to change the world by giving them away. Will you drink the cup?

Prayer

Jesus, the cup You offer us is bottomless, with opportunities to drink at every intersection, every chance meeting. In Your time upon this earth, You traversed a great area in order to show love to Your people. You were present in Your times, in Your discussions, in Your teachings and prayers. You looked into eyes and You reached into sore areas with tenderness and love. We believe we are called to drink from Your cup, that we are to overflow with Your grace into all areas of the world . . . in our homes, next door, and in our community, city, and beyond. Help us to walk Your path and abandon our own. Thank You for grace, love, and healing. Amen.

ANA MARIA IN ECUADOR

Ana Maria lives with her parents in tropical Ecuador. Both of her parents find part-time work as day laborers, doing anything they can to earn money. On most days Ana Maria will eat beans, bananas, and fish. Because of high unemployment, crime is a big problem and the community is considered a dangerous place to live. Ana Maria helps at home by making beds, running errands, and cleaning. She is young and is a bright student. Pray that as she grows, God will protect Ana Maria from violence and that there will be peace in her home. Pray that job opportunities will improve and basic nutrition and health care will become more affordable.

Day 40

As painful as the Friday of Jesus's crucifixion must have been for His disciples and friends, the morning after must have been even more challenging. We all know what it feels like to fail our friends and family, but we can only imagine the despair the disciples felt as they contemplated their failure to be with their friend in His darkest hour. They had been confident and sure Jesus was the Messiah, the one they had been waiting for. Yet the day after His crucifixion, they must have felt foolish as they came to grips with the reality that He was just another failed messiah.

On this Saturday the disciples waited in darkness, just as Jesus was enclosed in a dark tomb. I imagine they said very little to each other. What do you say in the midst of such suffering and pain? It has become common for people of faith to use phrases that are intended to bring comfort, like, "It is always darkest before the dawn." If we took a survey, we likely would find that many people believe this phrase comes from Scripture, but it does not. And besides that, it is not true on multiple levels. It's not true scientifically (it is darkest around midnight), and often it is not true in our lives either. Just because things get really dark does not mean they are going to get any better.

In one of my favorite books of the Bible and perhaps the most misunderstood, the book of Revelation, John had a vision on the Isle of Patmos that was intended for a group of Christians who were suffering profoundly. As they embraced faith in Jesus, they were tortured, persecuted, and killed. If I had to summarize the book of Revelation in one word, it would be "hope." John speaks a word of hope, and yet it is a peculiar hope. John does not say things will get better; in fact, he seems to imply things will get much worse. But in Revelation 21 he asks his readers to fix their eyes not on the end of their suffering but on a day that is coming—an eternity where they (and we) will know the fullness of God's love and grace.

I looked again *and could hardly believe my eyes*. Everything above me was new. Everything below me was new. *Everything around me was new* because the heaven and earth that had been had passed away, and the sea was gone, completely. And I saw the holy city, the new Jerusalem, descending out of heaven from God, prepared like a bride *on her wedding day*, adorned for her husband *and for His eyes only*. And I heard a great voice, coming from the throne.

A Voice: See, the home of God is with *His* people.
He will live among them;
They will be His people,
And God Himself will be with them.
The prophecies are fulfilled:
He will wipe away every tear from their eyes.
Death will be no more;
Mourning no more, crying no more, pain no more,
For the first things have gone away.

And the One who sat on the throne announced *to His creation,*

The One: See, I am making all things new. (turning to me) Write *what you hear and see*, for these words are faithful and true.[54]

Just as John encouraged these dear souls to fix their eyes on heaven, Paul calls the church in Colossae to do the same.

So *it comes down to this:* since you have been raised with the Anointed One, *the Liberating King*, set your mind on heaven above. The Anointed is there, seated at God's right hand. Stay focused on what's above, not on earthly things, because your *old* life is dead and gone. Your *new* life is now hidden, enmeshed with the Anointed who is in God. On that day when the Anointed One—who is our very life—is revealed, you will be revealed with Him in glory![55]

The darkness surrounding the disciples on this day is not unfamiliar to us. We too have failed, and we too suffer the consequences of our failures. We know darkness. Our hope is not that a better day is just around the corner. It may be—it may not be. Our hope is that Jesus is preparing a place for us in eternity, where all things will be made right. If in the days that follow, we become, as the disciples did, a people who fix their eyes on eternity, the suffering of the present is not nearly as painful because it is overshadowed by a deeper and larger purpose.

Prayer

God, on days where we are stunned with grief, give us a sense of the heartache Your disciples must have felt at being severed from their Teacher. Help us to face You, even when darkness lays heavy upon us. May we remember that You have our eternal home in order, ready and waiting when the time comes. In the meantime, may we become a people who live well regardless of our circumstances. May we learn to be content in good times as well as in seasons that are marked by pain and suffering. Forgive us when we fail to wait patiently, and teach us when we lack knowledge. Amen.

DUCET IN HAITI

Ducet is a Haitian man who survived the 7.0 magnitude earthquake in January 2010. When the earthquake hit, he sprinted home as fast as he could only to find his house had collapsed in shambles. He called into the chaos and heard his young daughter shout back to him as well as another woman. Digging in the wrong place could result in the rubble collapsing further, crushing his daughter. He carefully began to remove the remains of his house until he opened a hole large enough for the other woman to come through. His daughter grabbed on to her ankle, and Ducet pulled both of them to safety. In the midst of losing his home and having to care for his family, Ducet, who works with Living Water, continued serving his neighbors the very next day by repairing broken hand pumps in his community. The average income in Haiti is less than $360/year, and the vast majority of Haitians do not have access to clean water. Today, let's remember Ducet, his family, and Haiti—nearly 8 million people who are simply trying to survive.

FEAST DAY: Celebrating Forgiveness

We have paused for 40 days to connect with the poor and to go on our own exodus journey—out of our sin, out of our selfishness. In doing so, we have learned things about ourselves that we would have never learned otherwise. In some areas we experienced breakthrough as we ceased compulsive behaviors or let go of anger and bitterness. In other areas we continue to struggle. In these areas we anticipate fighting the good fight for the rest of our lives—and we will not always be victorious. Do not let that discourage you; ultimately we will know victory.

Today is not a day to contemplate our sin; it is a day to celebrate forgiveness and the power of the resurrection. We, like Paul, have been exposed: our sin is evident and we acknowledge that we have no righteousness of our own. So we cling to the one true source of righteousness and experience true resurrection power:

> But whatever I used to count as my greatest accomplishments, I've written them off as a loss because of the Anointed One. And more so, I now realize that all I gained *and thought was important* was nothing but yesterday's garbage compared to knowing the Anointed Jesus, my Lord. For Him I have thrown everything aside—*it's nothing but a pile of waste*—so that I may gain Him. *When it counts,* I want to be found belonging to Him, not clinging to my own righteousness based on law, but actively relying on the faithfulness of the Anointed One. *This is true* righteousness, supplied by God, acquired by faith.

I want to know Him *inside and out*. I want to experience the power of His resurrection and join in His suffering, shaped by His death, so that I may arrive *safely* at the resurrection from the dead.[56]

The resurrection changes everything; it brings light into the depths of darkness, gives us hope amid despair, and removes the sting of death. Today is a day to worship God, eat good food, celebrate with friends and family, and focus our hearts on God's love and goodness. Today is a day to embed in our memories, so we can remember the joy of the Lord in times of hardship and remember these words about the resurrection and its power in our lives.

Friends, it is this same might and *resurrection* power that He used in the Anointed One to raise Him from the dead and to position Him at His right hand in heaven. *There is nothing over Him*. He's above all rule, authority, power, and dominion; over every name invoked, *over every title bestowed* in this age and the next. God has placed all things beneath His feet and anointed Him as the head over all things for His church. This church is His body, the fullness of the One who fills all in all.[57]

It has been a remarkable blessing to share this journey with you. Thank you. Let us close in prayer, using the words of the apostle Paul to his community in Ephesus.

Prayer

God of our Lord Jesus, the Anointed, Father of Glory: *I call out to You on behalf of Your people*. Give them a mind ready to receive wisdom and revelation so they will truly know You. Open the eyes of their hearts, *and let the light of Your truth flood in*. Shine Your light on the hope You are calling them to embrace. Reveal to them the glorious riches You are preparing as their inheritance. Let them see the full extent of Your power that is at work in those of us who believe, and may it be done according to Your might and power.

Friends, it is this same might and *resurrection* power that He used in the Anointed One to raise Him from the dead and to position Him at His right hand in heaven. *There is nothing over Him.* He's above all rule, authority, power, and dominion; over every name invoked, *over every title bestowed* in this age and the next. God has placed all things beneath His feet and anointed Him as the head over all things for His church. This church is His body, the fullness of the One who fills all in all.[58]

Conclusion

Walking Onward

I want to take a moment to congratulate you on accomplishing what most would consider a spiritual marathon. Over the course of this experience you have likely developed a different cadence or rhythm—in life and in your interactions with God.

We did not fast perfectly. I'm not sure what a perfect fast even looks like. Our spiritual journeys are filled with ups and downs, and we likely can remember moments when we were distracted during this fast, when our eyes drifted from Jesus. Our attention and affection were at times focused less on Scripture and prayer and more on our own goals and ambitions for this life. But stumbling along the way reminds us of our imperfections and constant need for God.

The success of this fast is not based on how well we kept the rules during the fast, how much weight we lost, or how much time we spent in prayer. The real success of this fast comes in the ways our lives have been changed. It is quite possible that we will never see food in the same way again—that when we eat, we will feel a sense of gratitude to God for what He has provided, and a sense of connection to the poor. It is also possible this connection will lead us to pray more often for those in desperate need and to give

219

in ways that will transform the world. If so, I would call this a fast that pleases God.

In James 2, the brother of Jesus wants to make it very, very clear that in order to live the life of faith, we are called to action.

> Brothers and sisters, it doesn't make any sense to say you have faith and act in a way that denies that faith. *Mere talk never gets you very far, and* a commitment to Jesus only in words will not save you. It would be like seeing a brother or sister without any clothes *out in the cold* and begging for food, and saying, "Shalom, *friend,* you should get inside where it's warm and eat something," but doing nothing about his needs—*leaving him cold and alone on the street.* What good would your words alone do? The same is true with faith. Without actions, *faith is useless. By itself,* it's *as good as* dead. I know what you're thinking: "OK, you have faith. And I have actions. Now let's see your faith without works, and I'll show you a faith that works." Do you think that just believing there's one God is going to get you anywhere? The demons believe that too and it terrifies them! *The fact is,* faith has to show itself through works performed in faith. If you don't recognize that, then you're an empty soul.
>
> Wasn't our father Abraham made right with God by laying his son Isaac on the altar? The faith *in his heart* was made known in his behavior. In fact, his commitment was perfected by his obedience. That's what Scripture means when it says, "Abraham entrusted himself to God, and God credited him with righteousness." *And living a faithful life* earned Abraham the title of "God's friend." *Just like our father in the faith,* we are made right with God through good works, not simply by what we believe or think. Even Rahab the prostitute was made right with God by hiding the spies and aiding in their escape. Removing action from faith is like removing breath from a body. All you have left is a corpse.[1]

After 46 days of prayer, contemplation, fasting, and celebration, I read these words of James and feel a burning in my soul to do something, to be a part of something unique and beautiful. I hope this newfound connection with God and the poor will lead us to form new friendships. The world is filled with hard-working people living lives of despair because they lack food, water, and medical care. And as we learn to share our plenty and develop true and meaningful relationships with brothers and sisters across the globe, we will find our own salvation. Do you remember the story of Jesus and the short man, Zacchaeus? When he finally began to give away the riches he hoarded, salvation came to . . . whom? Those in need? No. Salvation came to Zacchaeus.

God is calling you to action. It might be to sponsor a child through an organization like Compassion International or to pool your resources throughout the year to sponsor a well through Living Water International. Or at the local level, you might share a meal with the poor. At Ecclesia we encourage our members not to only serve food to the poor but to eat with them, to feast together, to eat the same food. I believe it is in those places of equality, fellowship, and friendship that change happens on both ends of the table. I encourage you to dream big. To see the problems of this world, the devastation of extreme poverty, and the many global crises we face, and to believe that God is leading us as His people to be His restoring hands that bring healing to the suffering.

At the end of the day, our greatest calling is to love God and to love our neighbor. My greatest struggle is to take myself and my selfish desires and ambitions out of the way and to replace those selfish desires with the desires of God. To this end, I want to close with a beautifully meaningful prayer by Walter Brueggemann.

Ourselves at the Center
On reading 2 Samuel 7

We are your people,
    mostly privileged
        competent
        entitled.
Your people who make futures for ourselves,
        seize opportunities,
        get the job done
        and move on.

In our self-confidence, we expect little
    beyond our productivity;
    we wait little for
        that which lies beyond us,
    and then settle with ourselves
        at the center.

And you, you in the midst of our privilege,
            our competence
            our entitlement.

You utter large, deep oaths
    beyond our imagined futures.
    You say—fear not, I am with you.
    You say—nothing shall separate us.
    You say—something of new heaven and new
        earth.
    You say—you are mine; I have called you by name.
    You say—my faithfulness will show concretely
        and will abide.

And we find our privilege eroded by your purpose,
        our competence shaken by your future,
        our entitlement unsettled by your other
            children.

Give us grace to hear your promises.
Give us freedom to trust your promises.
Give us patience to wait and
    humility to yield our dreamed future
        to your large purpose.

        We pray in the name of Jesus who
        is your deep *yes* over our lives.[2]

A DVD Guide for Groups and Individuals

Session 1: Beginning . . .

1. What do you hope to learn during this 40-day journey? Do you have other hopes?
2. What are some of the obstacles that you foresee as you enter this fast? What are some healthy ways to respond when you slip up?
3. What are some ways you seek comfort, power, and strength in your life? How do these affect your life? How do they numb you from the injustices of those in need in the world?
4. What foods do you plan to eat during the 40 days?
5. How will you hold yourself and others accountable during the fast?
6. Have you ever taken a prayer walk? What are your thoughts about doing so during the 40 days?
7. How do you plan to celebrate the Sabbath during this fast?
8. What are your thoughts about how to remain humble during this fast?

Session 2: Things Sacred and Holy

1. How can we make defiled things holy and restore what is broken through Christ?
2. What are some places where you feel closest to the Lord? During the 40 days, what scheduling adjustments could you make to spend time in these places? What might you do in these places?
3. What needs to be destroyed in your life so that you can allow Jesus to reign fully in you?
4. How can you bring peace into the world around you?
5. How do you see heaven breaking loose on earth? How is God inviting you in that restoration?
6. What else in this video stood out to you, and why?

Session 3: The Meaning of Abundance

1. Compare your typical diet to that of those in developing countries. What feeling does this comparison give you?
2. You are likely at least two weeks into your fast by now. What are you learning from the experience?
3. In what ways do you open your table and life to the poor?
4. As you fast, what are some things you own that you feel are excessive?
5. How will you share from your abundance in this time?

Session 4: The Things We Trust

1. How do people you know plan for their old age and death? What do people like Anna do? What is our trust in, and what should it be in?
2. How can we intentionally plan our meals and lives in a way that we are regularly sharing our abundance?

3. How often do you have meals with the TV on? Discuss what you think a meal would look like with your friends and family when there are no distractions around?
4. James writes that if you have true faith, you will act upon it. How do you and how could you help those who are hungry and sick around you?
5. Discuss the joy that you think a sponsored child receives when she receives a handwritten letter from a sponsor or friend from the US.

Session 5: Trials and Tribulation

1. What might the significance of "Jerusalem" be to the people of Jerusalem, Haiti?
2. Discuss what it would be like to be on the Living Water International team that got their drill pipe stuck without finding any water. How does this story change your perspective about your own challenges?
3. Have you ever been camping? How many nights did you stay in the tent? Discuss what it would be like to stay with your entire family in that same tent for weeks, months, even years.
4. Jesus said, "Foxes have holes, the birds of the air have nests, but the Son of Man has no place to lay his head." What are the implications for how we view those who do not have access to safe shelter?
5. Could your church do something to provide clean water to those in need? How would that look, practically speaking?

Session 6: Life from Rocks

1. What lessons will you take with you from this fasting experience?
2. How will you continue this fast beyond the 40 days? What will you do differently with your budget or food intake? How might you raise awareness to get others involved?

3. How do you and your church pray for folks in need of basic things, such as food, water, and shelter?
4. Note the parallel between when the rock rolled away from Jesus' tomb and when a drill breaks enough rock to bring forth water. God is in the business of bringing life from rocks. What are the rocks in your life from which God can bring life?
5. What are the rocks in your community and the world to which you can direct life-giving attention?

Notes

Chapter 1: From Consuming to Sharing

1. 2 Corinthians 3:17.
2. This definition is from Merriam-Webster online, http://www.merriam-webster.com/dictionary/consume. I accessed it on August 27, 2011.
3. State of the World's Children, 2005, UNICEF.
4. "Log Cabin to White House? Not Any More," *The Observer*, April 28, 2002.
5. Shaohua Chen and Martin Ravallion, "The Developing World Is Poorer than We Thought, but No Less Successful in the Fight against Poverty," World Bank, August 2008.
6. Exodus 16:18.
7. 2 Corinthians 8:13–15.
8. Isaiah 58:6–10.
9. Alexander Roberts, James Donaldson, and Arthur Cleveland Coxe, eds., *The Pastor of Hermas, Bk. III*, in *The Ante-Nicene Fathers: The Writings of the Fathers Down to A.D. 325*, vol. 2, (New York: Cosimo, 2007).
10. Augustine of Hippo, quoted in Lynne M. Baab, *Fasting: Spiritual Freedom Beyond Our Appetites* (Downers Grove, IL: InterVarsity, 2006), 55–56.
11. http://economix.blogs.nytimes.com/2010/09/23/the-world-is-fat/.

Chapter 2: Miracle Bread

1. Numbers 11:1.
2. Numbers 11:4–9.
3. Numbers 11:10–23.
4. Numbers 11:23.
5. Numbers 11:31–35.

Chapter 3: Tools

1. Psalm 34:8.

2. Philippians 2:1–5.
3. Matthew 6:16.
4. Galatians 6:2–5.

Chapter 4: Fasting and Feasting

1. Psalm 46:10.
2. Mother Teresa to the Rev. Michael Van Der Peet, September 1979.
3. Mark 2:19.
4. Leviticus 19:34.
5. This poem is readily available in a number of places online and in books. It is sometimes referred to as the *Irish Rune of Hospitality*.
6. Hebrews 13:2.
7. Quote taken from episode six of *Iconoclast* on the Sundance Channel.

Daily Readings

1. Exodus 1:22.
2. *The Work of the People* video series with Walter Brueggemann, volume one.
3. Exodus 2:1–8.
4. Exodus 3:4–12.
5. Verses 28–30.
6. Exodus 4:1–17.
7. Matthew 15:29–38.
8. Luke 12:22–31.
9. This quote is widely attributed to G. K. Chesterton, but I do not know where it originally appeared.
10. Psalm 136:1–9.
11. Exodus 2:11–15.
12. Exodus 5:7–23.
13. A quote from the character Dr. Iannis, in Louis de Bernieres, *Corelli's Mandolin: A Novel* (New York: Vintage, 1995), 281 (originally published in Great Britain by Martin Secker & Warburg Limited, London, 1994).
14. Job 1:18–21.
15. Exodus 7:1–6.
16. Matthew 18:23–33.
17. Romans 6:19–23.
18. Exodus 14:1–13.
19. Isaiah 55:1–5.
20. Luke 10:1–3.
21. Exodus 14:13–31.
22. Exodus 15:1–19.
23. Exodus 12:1–14.
24. Exodus 16:1–4.
25. Exodus 17:1–6.
26. Luke 18:11.
27. Romans 7:15–20.

28. Numbers 11:1–10.
29. Numbers 12:1–14.
30. Exodus 18:6–11.
31. Leviticus 23:1–8.
32. Exodus 20:1–6.
33. Verses 1–15.
34. Exodus 20:17.
35. Psalm 139:13.
36. Matthew 5:38–48.
37. Philippians 4:10–13.
38. Exodus 20:12.
39. 6:1–4.
40. Exodus 20:7.
41. Exodus 20:8–11.
42. John 5:2–9.
43. Colossians 1:15–20.
44. Sarah Kirk and Weihua Li, "The Burden of Asthma in Texas: A Report from the Texas Asthma Control Program" (pdf available at http://www.dshs.state.tx.us/asthma/reports.shtm).
45. Acts 7:1–35.
46. Acts 7:36–60.
47. Romans 7:4–14.
48. Deuteronomy 32:36–43.
49. John 12:1–13.
50. Luke 7:22–23.
51. John 12:23–33.
52. John 13:1–17.
53. Matthew 20:20–24.
54. Revelation 21:1–5.
55. Colossians 3:1–4.
56. Philippians 3:7–11.
57. Ephesians 1:19–23.
58. Ibid.

Conclusion

1. James 2:14–26
2. Walter Brueggemann, *Prayers for a Privileged People* (Nashville: Abingdon, 2008), 46.

Chris Seay is a pastor, speaker, and author. In 1999 he planted a missional church, Ecclesia, with his wife, Lisa, and brother, Robbie, in Houston's Montrose district, the most challenging neighborhood in the city. Ecclesia (www.ecclesiahouston.org) is a unique community that is living out the gospel in compelling ways, in Houston and across the globe. The church's home base, 2115 Taft Street, houses Taft Street Coffee (an all fair trade coffee shop rated as one of the top three coffee shops in the city by AOL Citysearch), a bookstore, an organic food market (Central City Co-op, www. centralcityco-op.org), a recording studio (www.hydeparkstudio. com), an art gallery (www.xnil.org), a music venue, and a score of other community events. A community center on week days, the venue transforms into a place of worship on Sundays as over a thousand people cram themselves into this small urban space to celebrate the love of Christ.

Chris's vision for a new translation of the Bible goes back twenty years to his early attempts to teach the Bible as the story of God. As president of Ecclesia Bible Society, his vision culminated in *The Voice* (www.hearthevoice.com), a translation by both creatives and scholars that emphasizes narrative.

Chris has authored or coauthored many books, including *The Gospel According to Tony Soprano, The Gospel Reloaded, Faith of My Fathers, The Tao of Enron, The Gospel According to LOST, Advent Conspiracy,* and *The Gospel According to Jesus.*

CHILD SURVIVAL • SAFE WATER
CHILD PROTECTION • LIFESAVING FOOD • DISASTER RELIEF
EMERGENCY CARE • EDUCATION
THE LOVE OF JESUS

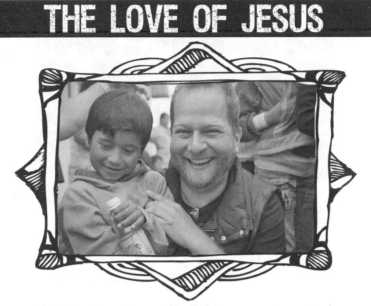

"God has given the world all the resources we need
for every person on the planet to thrive. I know
of no better way to share than to sponsor a child
through Compassion International."

— Chris Seay

Extreme poverty claims thousands of lives each day. Compassion
International is determined to fight this injustice. As the world's
leading child development ministry, Compassion offers hope to
more than 1.2 million children around the world. Babies, children,
and young adults in extreme poverty receive *life-changing* help.
And because Compassion works with Christ-centered churches in
developing countries, each child learns about God's amazing love.

LEARN HOW *YOU* CAN MAKE A DIFFERENCE AT
CHRISSEAY.NET

1 GROUP + 6 SESSIONS + 40 DAYS
= **RADICAL FAITH**

View Chris Seay Video

This six-session DVD, shot in locations such as the Holy Land, Haiti, and Ecuador, will help small groups and entire churches begin a passionate journey of radical faith, personal action, solidarity with the poor, and extravagant grace.

All your group or class needs is one six-session DVD and a copy of the softcover book for each person, which includes discussion questions.

Free Downloads and Samples at www.chrisseay.net